A DARK
HISTORY OF
BRISTOL

SWINDLES, SCANDALS, AND SKULDUGGERY

DEREK ROBINSON

COUNTRYSIDE BOOKS
NEWBURY BERKSHIRE

No reproduction permitted without the prior
permission of the publisher:

COUNTRYSIDE BOOKS
3 Catherine Road,
Newbury, Berkshire.

ISBN 1 85306 930 2
EAN 978185306 9307

Designed by Peter Davies, Nautilus Design
Produced through MRM Associates Ltd, Reading
Printed by Arrowsmith, Bristol.

CONTENTS

THANKS

to Jane Bradley and Dawn Dyer,
of the Local Studies Unit at
Bristol Central Library, for
digging deep into the archives
in search of illustrations;
and to Tony Osborne and Ray Glover,
for their photographic wizardry
which did the pictures a power
of good.

INTRODUCTION

1973 was a big year for Bristol. It marked six hundred years as a city *and* a county. Joy was unconfined. The thunder of self-congratulation was deafening. The city fathers danced in the streets. So many people tried to slap themselves on the back that casualty wards for miles around were full of dislocated shoulders.

Well, I didn't buy it. Not all of it, anyway. I'm a Bristolian, born and bred. I knew that, during the past six hundred years, the city and county had generated its fair share of blood and thunder. Also thud and blunder.

So I wrote this book, to help balance the story. I was not out to blacken Bristol's reputation. Some good things have happened here. Equally, you don't have to look hard to find bungling and swindling, cock-ups and carnage, ferocity and farce.

The book drew blood. A disgusted ratepayer, George Bodger, wrote to the *Western Daily Press* demanding that it be burned in the gutters. But Bristolians are a fair and level-headed lot. They know their history is like their geography: full of highs and lows. The true picture is the whole picture and this New Edition aims to offer nothing less.

Derek Robinson

Bristol's location near the Severn Estuary made it a major trader with Ireland, including (in early days) the export of white slaves. The ancient-looking map shows Shirehampton; it probably dates from 1670.

CHAPTER ONE

WHITE SLAVERY

L ong before Bristol made a fortune out of black slavery, the city ran a thriving business in white slavery.
Exactly when it began, nobody knows; but by the time of the Norman Conquest, Bristol was the most important centre in England for collecting, selling and exporting slaves (especially attractive young women). In those days the actual practice of slavery was fairly common everywhere. Even clergy kept slaves to run their farms, and by Anglo-Saxon law a poor man was allowed to sell his son into slavery for seven years, although exactly how the boy was supposed to regain his freedom at the end of that term was never explained.

The difference between Bristol and the rest of the country was that Bristol turned white slavery into big business. Local traders bought men and women all over England and exported them to many parts of Europe, but especially to Ireland. It became the fashion for an Irishman with any social ambitions to keep at least one English slave. Bristol ships ran a shuttle service, swapping English people for Irish goods.

A writer of the times described the scene on the quays in Bristol. 'Ranks of wretched persons bound together with ropes ... daily brought to market, daily sold.' He also noticed the shrewd commercial approach of the Bristol businessmen: 'The young women they commonly got with child, and carried them off to market in their pregnancy, that they might bring a better price.' Two for the price of one, in fact. The whole slave-trading operation was run so slickly, and brought in such a good living, 'that neither the love of God nor King William had hitherto been able to abolish it'. Not that the king made much of an effort; he was getting a good cut in the form of duty on every slave sold.

The man who rocked the boat was Wulfran, Bishop of Worcester. Bristol was in his diocese, and he visited the place to see for himself how the slave trade was carried on. The commercial inhumanity of it all shocked him into starting a one-man campaign to stamp it out: a brave act, roughly comparable with trying to convert Smithfield Market to vegetarianism. Wulfran lived in Bristol for months at a time and preached against slavery every Sunday.

Astonishingly, he began to wear the citizens down. At about the same time, Lanfranc, who was Archbishop of Canterbury, was working on King William to do without the slave-duty. Both appeals succeeded. Bristol renounced the slave trade and William forbade it – which is not to say that it came to an end. A hundred years later, when Henry II invaded Ireland, he found great numbers of English slaves. Some had been sold to the Irish by pirates and outlaws, but many came from Bristol traders, who could still buy children from their parents in the market place and ship them overseas like young cattle.

For as long as anyone could remember, Ireland had been one of Bristol's best customers, so it must have come as a shock when, in 1172, Henry granted 'to my men of Bristowe my city of Dublin for them to inhabit'. His idea was to colonize Dublin by letting Bristol take it over and run the place, as he hoped, 'well and peaceably, freely and quietly'. So many Bristolians moved to Dublin that the Dubliners were driven across the Liffey and up into the mountains. These former owners of English slaves were not happy with the new arrangement. They raided the town vigorously and often, and when on Easter Monday in 1209 they caught the Bristol colonists holidaymaking at Killin Woods outside Dublin, the Irish had a bloody holiday of their own. Few of their enemies made it back through the gates of Dublin. The slaughter was so great that reinforcements had to be sent out from Bristol. Black Monday was commemorated for many years thereafter, with much parading of troops, waving of banners, and issuing of challenges – which the Irish took up, in their own sweet time, and finally won their Dublin back again.

White-slaving was easy and profitable, and Bristolians never really lost the taste for it, especially when the new colonies of North America and the West Indies opened up a splendid, expanding market.

In August 1648 – during the Civil War – Cromwell defeated the king's Scottish army in Lancashire and took thousands of prisoners. Promptly, 'the gentlemen of Bristol applied to have liberty to transport 500 of the prisoners to the plantations'. The request was granted, and 500 Scottish slaves were shipped from Bristol to live, work and die on the big estates in Jamaica or Virginia, many of them owned by Bristolians. After another royalist defeat at Worcester in 1651, more Scots prisoners went down the Avon to be transported into slavery. In July 1652 it was the turn of the Irish. The Council of State ordered the Governor of Waterford to deliver to three Bristol merchants as many Irish prisoners as they wanted for the West Indies; and three months later another merchant took collection of 200 Irishmen for sale in Barbados.

These businessmen were obviously on to a good thing; the end of the war must have come as a disappointment to them. There was, however, an alternative source of slaves: kidnapping. In 1654, Bristol Corporation passed an ordinance 'to prevent the kidnapping of boys, maids and others and transporting them beyond seas and there disposing of them for private gain'. This sounded good, and it probably stifled a few complaints from indignant parents; but the fact was that the 'private gain' went into the pockets of the same merchants who had voted for the ordinance in the Council Chamber and who then took their seats on the Bench to make sure that it wouldn't work. Occasionally they convicted a man of kidnapping and ordered him to be pilloried, which could be a severe penalty if the mob pelted him hard and accurately enough; but invariably the justices added the words *to be protected*. This meant that the prisoner was allowed to hire thugs to hang around the pillory and look discouragingly at anyone who turned up with a rotten cabbage in his hand. The sentence was frivolous.

All the same, kidnapping was a crude and clumsy way to recruit slave labour, and the magistrates soon developed a much smoother technique.

It was not unusual for a criminal to have a severe sentence (such as hanging) reduced to transportation for life, and since the aldermen and justices of the peace all traded with the American colonies, they naturally sold the convict to any plantation-owner who needed a good (or even a bad) man. It was a rewarding trade – no expenses, all profit – and the city fathers found a way to make it even better.

The mayor and justices usually met at noon at the tolsey (a courthouse conveniently near the merchants' meeting-place) in order to hear any charges that might have come up since yesterday. The men brought before them were mostly small-time swindlers and pilferers. The magistrates gave each prisoner such a grilling that he was soon shaking in his shoes. At this point, one of the officers of the court would murmur some advice in his ear, such as: 'Take my tip, cully, and put in a plea for transportation, otherwise they'll stretch your neck just like they did that bloke last Tuesday. Or was it Wednesday?'

It was a brave prisoner who ignored this advice (especially as petty criminals were sometimes hanged anyway) so the tolsey produced a steady supply of manpower. The spoils were distributed to the aldermen in strict rotation, and although a few of the rich men passed up their chance, they all connived at the racket. Indeed, by 1685 it was such an established routine that the justices regarded it almost as one of the perks of the job.

The significance of 1685 is that it was the year when Lord Chief Justice Jeffreys came west to hold his Bloody Assize.

His mission was to punish the rebels who had supported Monmouth's rebellion, and he spared neither himself nor them. In Devon and Somerset he had 233 prisoners hanged, quartered and gibbeted. Twelve were executed in Pensford, eleven at Keynsham. Jeffreys also sentenced about 850 to transportation as slaves to the West Indies, and it's interesting to see how well he knew their market value. He advised the king (James II) that they were in great demand and that His Majesty should therefore take care over deciding who got them, because they were worth £10 a head, if not £15. No doubt a few Bristol merchants were licking their lips, but James gave the prisoners to his queen and some of his courtiers to sell.

Jeffreys then moved to Bristol and opened the assize at the Guildhall. He was in a foul temper when he arrived – he suffered from kidney stones and drank steadily in an effort to kill the pain – and the small number of rebels in the dock made him angrier. Six death sentences and several lashings were the most he could achieve. Jeffreys had never trusted Bristol, and this poor showing confirmed his blackest suspicions. After a series of blistering remarks he became impatient with his own moderation: 'Come, come, gentlemen,' he snapped, 'to be plain with you I find the dirt of the ditch in your nostrils. Good God! Where am I? In *Bristol?*'

The mayor, Sir William Hayman, and the aldermen were present in court, all gorgeously robed, and Jeffreys decided to give them a lick with the rough side of his tongue.

'Sir!' he barked. 'Mr Mayor, you I mean, kidnapper! And that old Justice on the bench' – pointing at Alderman Lawford – 'an old knave – he goes to the tavern, and for a pint of sack he will bind people servants to the Indies. A kidnapping knave! I will have his ears off, before I go forth of town.'

Clearly, Jeffreys knew all about the Bristol justices' racket. He flung a paper at the Town Clerk and ordered him to read it. The court – half of them fascinated, the other half terrified – listened to a detailed account of several kidnappings, culminating in an attempt by the mayor to have an alleged pickpocket transported for life.

Jeffreys exploded with rage. 'Kidnapper!' he shouted. 'Do you see the keeper of Newgate? If it were not in respect of the sword which is over your head, I would send you to Newgate, you kidnapping knave! You are worse than the pickpocket who stands at the bar. I hope you are men of worth. I will make you pay sufficiently for it!' And he did: he fined Hayman £1,000 on the spot. That sum was worth at least £200,000 in today's money, so it is safe to assume that the mayor reeled a little.

But worse (or better) was to come. Jeffreys disposed of some routine business, and the court – with a feeling of relief – was just getting ready for the midday adjournment when the Lord Chief Justice abruptly ordered the mayor into the prisoner's dock and told him to plead: guilty or not guilty?

For a moment the mayor – Sir William Hayman, chief citizen of Bristol, second city of the kingdom – was dumbfounded. The idea that he should enter the box so recently occupied by those sullen and unwashed criminals whose only distinction was their incompetence to avoid capture: it utterly astonished him. And how could he plead when he hadn't been charged, when he was still stunned at the thought of being charged at all? His Worship could only blink and hesitate.

This provoked new heights of fury. Jeffreys bawled at him and cursed, he stamped his feet until the dust rose, he even shouted for his soldiers. The king had commissioned him a general in case he ever needed force to back up his legal powers, and this looked like a good opportunity.

The mayor woke up and hurried into the box. In an apologetic voice he pleaded 'not guilty'. To the astonishment of the crowded courtroom, Jeffreys ordered the mayor to provide bail for his own re-appearance that same afternoon, and then committed him to the custody of the city sheriffs. And just in case Hayman thought he was being hard done by, Jeffreys put him straight.

'Had it not been in respect of the city,' the judge thundered, 'I would have arraigned him, and hanged him, before I went forth, and would have seen it done myself; a kidnapping knave!' Then he charged five other eminent Bristolians with kidnapping and adjourned for lunch, slightly less dissatisfied with the morning's work.

It would be comforting to think that the mayor and his five kidnapping colleagues were tried, convicted, and experienced a little of the suffering which they had inflicted on so many petty crooks who sweated out their lives as slaves on the other side of the Atlantic. Such justice rarely happened in England 300 years ago, and it certainly didn't happen in Bristol in this case. The trial was repeatedly adjourned on one trivial pretext after another until finally the charges were quietly dropped. Jeffreys' sulphurous performance in the Guildhall had been just that: a performance, a theatrical exercise to relieve his spleen and a savage demonstration that even mayors should go in fear of him; with a hangover and an alcoholic breakfast to give the show some zip.

The mayor and his friends paid for their offence, but they paid in cash, and discreetly. For all his crusading zeal to punish disloyalty, Jeffreys preferred to hang only the poor rebels and sell pardons to the rich ones. He took a large fortune out of the West Country. One example alone indicates the scale of his demands: Prideaux, son of a former Recorder of Bristol, paid him £15,000, worth at least £3,000,000 today. No doubt the mayor, too, paid Jeffreys dearly.

Not that Jeffreys got much joy from his riches. His only real pleasure lay in bolstering up the power of James II; and when, three years after the Bloody Assize, James fled the country, Jeffreys tried to follow him.

By this time the Lord Chief Justice – crippled by stomach pain and pickled with drink – was the most hated man in England. He disguised himself as a sailor but someone recognized him as he was drinking in a tavern in Wapping, and he was lucky to be arrested: lucky because if the mob had got there first they would have kicked him to death. He was escorted under guard to London and taken to the Lord Mayor, who fainted clean away when he saw him. At Jeffreys' own request he was put in the Tower. Thirty-five thousand guineas and a great deal of silver were found on board the Wapping collier on which he had planned to escape.

Arrangements were made to bring him to trial, and no doubt Sir William Hayman was not the only man in England looking forward to seeing the former Lord Chief Justice standing in his own dock and being asked how he chose to plead. But Jeffreys got in first with the most effective adjournment ever devised. On 18th April 1689, he died. He was 41.

CHAPTER TWO

QUAKER-BASHING

'These monsters are more numerous in Bristol
than in all the West of England. . .'

The history of religion in this country should be drawn in grey, flecked with crimson. It is largely a record of rabid intolerance, punctuated by fits of sadistic savagery. Bristol's contribution is not large, but what it lacks in quantity it makes up in ferocity.

In 1553 Mary Tudor was crowned Queen of England. Overnight, the Protestant faith became highly dangerous. Mary was a hard-line Roman Catholic, and by God she was determined to get England back into the Pope's orbit. The authorities in Bristol were not slow to please her. Mary succeeded to the throne in July. By October a martyr was burning on St Michael's Hill.

The man was William Shapton, a weaver, and the record simply says that he 'was burnt for religion'. The man who got the credit for his execution was John Griffith, one of the sheriffs, 'a very forward man' in sniffing out unorthodox believers. Before long he caught two more: Richard Sharp, also a weaver, who lived in Temple parish; and Thomas Hale, a shoemaker. Sharp was interrogated and 'persuaded' to recant, but it was a forced conversion and later on he said so, in public. He and Thomas Hale were taken to the stake on the top of St Michael's Hill. They shook hands and then were bound back-to-back and burned in the same fire.

A shearman, Thomas Benion, refused to believe that the sacrament of the altar – that is, the communion wafer and wine – actually and physically changed into the body and blood of Christ; he too was burned. (Highbury Chapel, in Cotham, now stands on the site.) And there is a report that two others 'suffered the fire for the profession of the gospel of Jesus Christ in Bristoll': Edward Sharp, a Wiltshire man, aged 60, and – ironically – a young carpenter, name unknown.

More would have died, but they escaped before they could be arrested. Mary herself died before they could be tracked down, and Queen Elizabeth put a stop to all religious executions (unless they had a political base, that is). Half a dozen burnings is not a lot, but it's the thought that counts, and the evidence suggests that Bristolians were pretty bloody-minded, preferring their victims to die as slowly as possible. Two local preachers, Pacy and Huntingdon, came back from exile when Elizabeth succeeded to the throne, and Huntingdon preached a scathing sermon from the cross on College Green. It's obvious that his listeners knew what – and who – he was talking about.

'Know ye not who made the strict search for Mr Pacy?' Huntingdon thundered. 'Whom if God had not hid, as Jeremiah, you had burned, stump and all!' (Pacy was a cripple.) 'Yet you had no pity,' he went on. 'And who you know went to Redland to buy *green* wood for the execution of those blessed saints that suffered; when near home, at the Back or Quay, he might have had *dry* . . .' The martyrs he was talking about were Sharp and Hale. Tudor punishments were never humane, but deliberately to linger over the burning of two men by making sure that the fire smouldered is to make a science out of cruelty.

In any case the persecution failed. Nonconformists of one kind or another flourished in Bristol, and in the early 1650s Quakerism began to attract a following. The Quakers too went through suffering and had their own martyrs; yet their church came through the ordeal stronger than ever. Mind you, in the beginning they more than asked for trouble; they demanded it.

The Quakers of 200 years ago were a rumbustious lot. They were filled to overflowing with that cocky certainty which comes from sudden conversion, and they didn't care where it spilled out. They interrupted church services, they denounced ministers, they contradicted Anglican teachings, they often made worship impossible with their wild disturbances. And they did it all in a ranting, raucous style which made their self-righteousness doubly hard to take. To cause a commotion in church was provocative enough; to insult respectable folk with torrents of hectic abuse was just too much – even if it was done in order to save their immortal souls.

The wonder is that the Quakers got away with it at first. In 1652, for instance, Sarah Goldsmith wrapped herself in sackcloth

(which exposed her legs: highly improper), covered her flowing hair with ashes, and paraded herself through all the Gates of the city, accompanied by two girl friends. When they reached the High Cross she exhibited herself 'as a sign against the pride of Bristol'. Not surprisingly she attracted a crowd; as usual they got out of hand; luckily for Sarah the magistrates rescued her before she got beaten up. She thanked them with a harangue. They put her in Bridewell to cool off.

Sarah Goldsmith was dotty, and harmless to nobody but herself. James Naylor, a Yorkshire Quaker who turned up in Bristol on 24th October 1656, was also off his head. He too made a spectacle of himself, but he said nothing critical of Bristol. Nevertheless he was punished with a savagery which could easily have killed him.

It was a very wet day, the 24th of October. Naylor had come up from Somerset with six friends. He went through Bedminster on horseback, one bareheaded friend in the lead, another bareheaded friend at the horse's head, the rest walking in escort, and all except Naylor singing *Holy, holy, holy, Lord God of Sabbath.*

The weather grew worse, but Naylor's friends deliberately walked in the worst part of the track. People watching saw them go through mud up to the knees. They sang the same chant all the way to the High Cross in the centre of Bristol, and then all the way to the White Hart in Broad Street. What sort of reception they expected nobody knows, but you can't re-enact Palm Sunday in the middle of a town without causing comment, even on a rainy day. The magistrates sent for them and had them locked up.

It was clear that Naylor's followers thought he was Jesus Christ. One of them, a woman called Dorcas Ebury, claimed that he had raised her from the dead; another had written him letters which contained such phrases as, 'Oh thou fairest of ten thousand, thou only begotten son of God . . .'. What Naylor thought he was, is less clear. When the magistrates examined him he repeatedly replied that he claimed nothing for himself except that which God had guided and directed in him. Finally they came to the point and asked him if he was the everlasting Son of God. Naylor should have stuck to his formula. Instead he said: 'Where God is manifest in the flesh, there is the everlasting Son, and I do witness God in the flesh. I am the Son of God, and the Son of God is but one.'

Well, that was enough. The magistrates sent Naylor to Parliament, together with all their reports. Parliament set up a committee to try him, and after a long trial he was found guilty of 'horrid blasphemy'. The question of his sentence now moved back to the House of Commons. They debated Naylor's punishment, if you can believe it, for *thirteen days*. A motion to have him put to death was narrowly defeated, 96 votes to 82. The actual sentence was almost as bad, and before it was over there must have been many people – Quakers included – who thought he would have suffered less on the gallows.

The sentence was in three parts: two in London and one in Bristol. The first part was carried out on 18th December 1656.

Naylor was placed in the pillory at Westminster and left to stand there for two hours. He was then taken out and whipped from Westminster to the Royal Exchange in the City of London. He received 310 lashes – one for each gutter he crossed on the way. This completed the first part.

Naylor was not a firebrand; he was not a revolutionary. He was a crackpot, and for that offence 310 lashes seemed enough. Many eminent Londoners were shocked by his treatment and they petitioned Parliament to set aside the rest of his sentence. Unfortunately for Naylor, Parliament was also getting petitions from other parts of the country, complaining of Quaker troublemaking. The Corporation of Bristol sent a petition urging Parliament 'to restrain the insolencies of these people' and accusing Naylor of being a ringleader of Bristol Quakers. This was totally false – Naylor scarcely knew them – but it destroyed any chance of mercy in the House of Commons. On 27th December he got the second part of his sentence.

It began where the first part left off: outside the Royal Exchange. At noon he was put in the pillory. What happened then is not for the squeamish:

'...he having stood till two, the executioner took him out, and having bound his arms with cords to the pillory, and having put a cap over his eyes, he bad him put forth his tongue, which he freely did, and the executioner with a red-hot iron about the size of a quill, bored the same, and by order from the Sheriff held it in a small space, to the end the beholders might see and bear witness, that the sentence was thoroughly executed; then having took it out and pulling the cap off that covered his face, he put a handkerchief over his eyes, and putting his left hand to the back part of his head, and taking the red-hot iron letter in his other hand put it to his forehead, till it smoaked: all which time James (Naylor) never so much as winced, but bore it all with astonishing and heart-melting patience. Being unbound, he took the executioner in his arms, embracing and hugging him ....

'This was also very remarkable, that notwithstanding there might be many thousands of people, yet they were very quiet, few heard to revile him, or seen to throw any one thing at him, and when he was burning, all the people both before him and behind him and on both sides of him with one consent stood bareheaded.'

The flogging and branding of James Naylor. Parliament debated for thirteen days before sentencing him to be whipped through London, branded, whipped through Bristol, and jailed.

23

After these tortures the journey from London to Bristol in mid-winter must have been a punishment in itself. Naylor reached the city on 17th January. The third and final part of his sentence was immediately carried out.

First he was taken through Bristol on horse, bareback and facing the tail. Then he was led to the middle of Thomas Street, stripped, and tied to a carthorse. Thereafter the route was precisely described:

'In the market first whipped;
from thence to the foot of the bridge, there whipped;
thence to the middle of High Street, there whipped;
thence to the Tolzey, there whipped;
thence to the middle of Broad Street, there whipped;
and then turn into the Taylor's-hall, there release him from the cart-horse, and let him put on his clothes, and carry him thence to Newgate by Tower-lane the back way.'

For Naylor was still not free. He went back to London to serve a period of hard labour until Parliament decided to release him.

It looks as if even Bristol was sick of punishing Naylor by the time he came back to be whipped: a man called Jones, described as 'a coppersmith and ugly Quaker' was given permission 'to hold back the beadle's arm when striking' (always assuming that the beadle would let him). But this tiny piece of compassion came very late in the day. The fact that Naylor survived, and eventually lived in Bristol for a while, doesn't hide the horror of his persecution.

The Corporation and magistrates – in those days they were one and the same thing – concentrated all their hate of Quakers on to Naylor. He was never dangerous; he was a deluded, simpleminded booby whose head had been turned by hero-worship. He wrote and said a lot of harsh things about the clergy, but he wasn't convicted of harsh criticism. He was convicted of blasphemy. Of this he was guilty; but his real offence was Quakerism, and the sentence he suffered was meant for all Quakers.

Four years later, Bristol began a campaign to eliminate them and all other Dissenters. The hounding went on for over 25 years.

It began in 1660 because that was the year when Charles II was restored to the throne and the Anglican Church got back its authority as the official religion of England. The Government at once commissioned Richard Ellsworth to summon all the inhabitants of Bristol over the age of 16 and command them to take the oaths of allegiance and supremacy to the king as sole head of the church.

The Quakers and the Anabaptists refused. Their principles would not allow them to swear any oath, for or against anything or anybody. Ellsworth asked London for powers to imprison those who would not conform. 'These monsters are more numerous in Bristol than in all the West of England,' he complained, 'and hold meetings of 1,000 to 1,200, to the great alarm of the city.' He got his powers, and issued a proclamation which banned the holding of religious meetings by Dissenters. He caught 65 Quakers at a prayer meeting in a private house in High Street and threw them into Newgate; then he netted a further 125 in Temple Street – 190 extra prisoners in a gaol which was overcrowded at any time. Eventually they were released (a lady Quaker by the name of Margaret Fell had a curious influence on Charles II at that time) but it was a taste of the bitterness to come.

In September 1663, Sir John Knight was elected mayor, and the hunt was on again. The first thing he did was arrest two Nonconformist preachers on a charge of rioting (the evidence was that they had, without permission, gathered more than five persons together). They were convicted, fined £50 each, couldn't (or wouldn't) pay, and went to Newgate for nine months.

That was just a trial run. By 11th November, Knight (accompanied by a sheriff, Richard Streamer – another straining bloodhound) had raided every conventicle (as Dissenters' meeting-houses were known) and gaoled every Dissenting leader in Bristol. When, in February 1664, he got an official note of thanks – 'His Majesty bade me tell you how much satisfied he is of your care of the good government of his city' – Knight flexed his muscles and set about earning greater praise.

A German impression of Naylor's entry into the city; his followers are chanting Holy, Holy, Holy. The Naylor story spread far beyond England.

On Sunday 28th February he marched into a house in Broadmead and found 300 Quakers assembled for worship. He ordered them out. Fourteen refused to go; they ended the day in prison. The following Sunday he broke up the Baptists' meeting; the Sunday after that was the Independents' turn. He was reluctant to give up the good work, even temporarily, but duty called him to Westminster. Sir John was Bristol's M.P. as well as its mayor, and he went up to put his weight behind the Conventicle Bill. This proposed that any person convicted three times of attending a Dissenting place of worship could be transported for seven years, after his property had been confiscated to cover the shipping costs. Knight had high hopes of this Bill; he told the House of Commons that his goal was to transport 400 Quakers before his mayoralty was over. Bearing in mind Judge Jeffreys' remarks about Bristol mayors and their fondness for kidnapping, one wonders whether Knight's great appetite for religious conformity was sharpened by the prospect of profit. Four hundred Quakers is a lot of manpower.

The Conventicle Bill was passed, and Knight hurried back to Bristol with a troop of cavalry to help him. In July he caught 200 Quakers in Broadmead and arrested the lot. The preacher got three months, the rest were fined. All but nine refused to pay; they joined the preacher for a month. Before they were out, Knight had gaoled another 100 Quakers. He worked his way through the Sundays of August, searching, raiding, gaoling. When he made it impossible for Dissenters to meet in rooms they got together secretly in attics or cellars. Knight intensified the hunt, seized another 31, and sent them to Bridewell.

Conditions in Bristol's prisons had never been better than foul, but now the overcrowding made them appalling. In Bridewell 55 women shared only five beds. There was virtually no sanitation, the food was rubbish, and the smell was enough to make a visitor retch. Two women died; the cause of death was said to be 'the stench'. The diagnosis may not be medically precise, but it carries conviction.

In his year as mayor, Sir John Knight gaoled about 900 Quakers, Baptists, Presbyterians and other Dissenters. However, he failed to achieve his ambition of exporting the problem to the Colonies. In December 1664 he did succeed in getting three Quakers committed for transportation to Barbados and taken down to the ship *Mary Fortune* on the quay, but the crew wouldn't stand for it, and they were brought back. Another difficulty was the friction between Knight and Richard Ellsworth. Quaker-bashing was a good way to curry favour with the Government, and Ellsworth was jealous of Knight's success – so jealous that he wrote to London alleging that Knight was soft on Quakers and Baptists!

Sir John was followed as mayor by John Lawford, who kept up the standard of Quaker-bashing; then Lawford was succeeded by the Great Plague of 1665-6, and for a long time there were more urgent things to worry about. As usual, persecution had only strengthened the faith of the Dissenters and boosted their numbers. In 1688 the Quakers felt confident enough to set up a school for the children of poor members; John Tappin, the first schoolmaster, got £10 a year (which gives us some sort of yardstick by which to measure the fines of £20 *a month* with which Dissenters were soon to be hit). In 1669 a royal proclamation urged magistrates everywhere to hammer Dissent with the full force of the law, but the Bristol bench had no stomach for the fight. They gaoled one preacher, who then preached to enormous crowds through a grating in Newgate prison; after that they quit.

In 1670 the Quakers opened their new meeting-house, built on the remains of the old Dominican Friary in Broadmead and thereafter known as 'Quakers Friars'. It symbolized the failure of the Conventicle Act. The Government, determined to crush Dissent, passed harsher laws; but it was easier to change the law than to change the people. The mayor and aldermen slogged away, fining and gaoling, and getting precious little help from the parish constables.

What's more the Dissenters were learning how to survive. They cut trapdoors in the floors of their meeting-houses through which the preachers escaped before the officers could get in. To counter this, Bishop Ironside – an unbeatable name, that – hired spies to infiltrate Dissenting services and identify the worshippers, and the magistrates had the seats and pulpits ripped out. The Dissenters simply went on using their wrecked chapels, so the magistrates locked the chapels and set the Trained Bands (a sort of Home Guard) to guard them. The Trained Bands had as little enthusiasm as the parish constables. On Sunday 4th September 1670, the Quakers succeeded in breaking open the doors of their own building four times. Sixteen Quakers went to gaol for that. The magistrates seized their furniture, but nobody would buy it; they shut down their chapels, but the congregations went out and held services in the lanes and fields.

The mayor paid them an unintentional compliment in his report to London: ' . . . the numerous criminals of the several sects seem obstinate to tire out the magistracy, as well as affront them by threats, so that the face of things has a bad aspect. The factious party are more numerous than the loyal, and unite, though of different persuasions ....'

That was the crunch: the Dissenters had won the people over to their side. For a while it even looked as if they might win over the Corporation, too. In 1670 the Council rejected the alderman who was in line to be mayor – and whom the king wanted to be mayor – and elected instead Mr John Knight, cousin of the notorious Sir John but, by contrast, a well-known friend of Dissenters. Sir John turned purple and blasted the election, denouncing the lot of them as 'fanatics', his word for anyone outside the Church of England. King Charles ordered them to go back and elect his alderman. With much courage the Council stood by its decision; Mr Knight was sworn in.

Sir John raged off to London and laid charges against his cousin, who rapidly ended up in the Tower. On 10th February 1671, the king questioned him, said that he 'was pleased to overlook the fault committed at the election, but ordered that his instructions should be faithfully obeyed in future', which was all well and good but it didn't get Mr Knight out of the Tower. A month later he was still inside, despite pressure from the Council, and it was 20th April before he saw Bristol again. An escort of 235 horsemen came out to meet him and led him to a great public reception. Sir John

Knight, on the other hand, came in through the back streets.

For a couple of years there was an awkward lull. The prisons were still full of Quakers, yet it was possible for a Presbyterian and an Independent to get royal licences to preach in private homes. The lull ended with a bang in September 1674. Ralph Oliffe was elected mayor. He proceeded to make Sir John Knight look like St Francis of Assisi.

Oliffe was a loudmouth, a bag of wind, the landlord of the Three Tuns and a heavy drinker. He hated all Dissenters, and he had two sheriffs who drank his liquor and shared his views. By an unhappy coincidence, Bishop Carleton appeared in Bristol at the same time and announced a crusade to root out and destroy every conventicle in the city. The campaign was given a kind of formal launching at the quarter sessions, where the grand jury delivered a long, bad-tempered statement blasting all Dissenters as seditious fanatics. Carleton sat on the bench and applauded. He was entitled to applaud: he had packed the jury with high churchmen and he'd probably also written their statement; so it was very much his show.

He struck first at the Nonconformist ministers. The parish of St James contained four meeting-houses. Carleton used a churchwarden by the name of Hellier to lay charges against them under the Conventicle Acts. Three of the chapels pointed out that they had been licensed by the king. Carleton cursed them, rode to London and got Charles to cancel the licences. On 10th February 1675 he led a posse made up of four parsons, two aldermen, some army officers and a small mob, to Castle Green Chapel. The minister, John Thompson, was holding a service. Carleton not only arrested him, he also took charge of the prosecution. His courtroom style was direct and to the point: Thompson was a seditious villain and a rebel dog and he ought to stretch a halter. Thompson got six months. Within a week three other ministers joined him.

Six months may not sound a lot. In those days it was often worse than a life sentence, for it could be a death sentence. Newgate was a foul, stinking hole, a breeding-ground for epidemics. Thompson went down with gaol-fever. Doctors warned the justices that he would die if he stayed there, and his friends offered £500 security if he could be moved. Bishop Carleton strenuously opposed the idea, and John Thompson died in Newgate on 4th March 1675. Five thousand people attended his funeral in St Philip's churchyard. Carleton dismissed his death as the result of 'a surfeit', and sent Hellier out to break up more prayer meetings. This time the prisoners were thrown into the worst cells Newgate could offer, with nowhere to sit but on the wet earthen floor.

The more they were hounded, the stronger the Dissenters' spirit became; but the stiffer their resistance, the worse became the persecution. Sunday was the dangerous day. Mayor Oliffe and his musclemen met at the Three Tuns to get tanked up, and then roared off in search of prayer-meetings. The worshippers could not meet force with force, but they met it with guile, often successfully. The approach of mayor Oliffe's gang, or churchwarden Hellier's squad, would be signalled ahead, and Oliffe or Hellier would find the chapel entrance jammed with women. By the time they'd forced their way inside, the preacher would have gone through the trapdoor or out by a hidden exit. The mayor would find the congregation singing psalms: holding a prayer-meeting was an offence but psalm singing wasn't; and the more he shouted at them, the louder they sang. Sometimes Oliffe stamped out in a rage and then rushed back ten minutes later, hoping to take them by surprise; if he were really furious he might come back three or four times. He was invariably out-sung. As a variation on this, the congregation sometimes sat in complete silence for hours on end. (If anything, silence was even more infuriating than singing.) Sooner or later Oliffe gave up and the preacher came back, often speaking from behind a curtain in order to baffle any paid informers who might be trying to identify him.

But against men like Oliffe and Hellier and Carleton, guile was not always enough. They sent their bruisers to break up the gatherings of Dissenters and scatter the congregations, and these hired roughnecks used the fist and the boot freely. Spies infiltrated the chapels. If the mayor and the bishop couldn't get real evidence they used perjured evidence to send a steady stream of Dissenters to Newgate. Week after week their squads raided meetings and brought in groups of up to 50 Dissenters to be convicted on the farcical charge of rioting and get an automatic gaol sentence. The three ministers who had been imprisoned with John Thompson served their time and were back inside almost as soon as they were released, and for the same offence: preaching.

Eventually Oliffe's year as mayor dragged to a close. Hellier soldiered on, but the new mayor was not of his stripe, and in any case the enemy seemed inexhaustible. Early in 1676 a Baptist minister called Hardcastle finished his *second* gaol sentence of six months; on the day of his release, he preached. Hellier retired to get his strength back.

His chance came again in 1681, when yet another Sir John Knight – not to be confused with any previous John Knight – was made sheriff. Knight regarded Dissenters the way a farmer regards rats. He and Hellier made a fine pair.

As usual, the attack began with the arrest of all the Nonconformist leaders. By November 1681 every Dissenting minister plus about a hundred laymen were inside Newgate. Then began an intensive campaign to destroy their churches – both the buildings and the congregations.

In December Hellier recruited a smith and fourteen labourers and took them to the Presbyterian chapel. They broke in and wrecked the place. From there they moved to the Baptists' meeting-house in Broadmead, and wrecked that. It was a short walk to Quakers Friars, and this too they wrecked. Despite the destruction the Baptists met at Broadmead on Boxing Day. The mayor and sheriffs in person turned up and sent the entire congregation to gaol. Within a few days every Nonconformist chapel in Bristol had been wrecked, and more members were in gaol. The Conventicle Act did not apply to children, and Hellier found many youngsters holding prayer-meetings of their own while their parents were doing time. He pleaded with the magistrates to have them lashed with the cat; instead they were put in the stocks and beaten with whalebone rods.

Astonishingly, the Dissenters endured and persisted and even throve. When their chapels were smashed they met for worship in the fields, sometimes forming crowds of a thousand or fifteen hundred. The mayors stationed the Trained Bands at the city gates on Sunday mornings to keep the Dissenters in. They went out on Saturday night instead. By now Hellier was under-sheriff of Somerset, too, and he used his authority to send patrols through the countryside near Bristol to hunt out open-air services.

Brislington Common was a useful rendezvous for Dissenters because it was close to the river; if Hellier's men appeared, they could dodge into Gloucestershire. On 11th April 1682 this bolt-hole turned into a trap. Hellier and the Somerset justices spotted a gathering of 200 in a dip on the Common, and grabbed nine of them. The rest got away and crossed the Avon to Crew's Hole – only to be cut off by another patrol led by the mayor and a Gloucestershire J.P. Many turned and struggled back across the Avon. A draper named Ford was drowned; the preacher – yet another Knight – managed to drag himself out, but he died later from exhaustion. Charles II found the incident amusing. It was no joke in Bristol.

Hellier had so many search parties out that he couldn't fail to make a huge number of arrests. The juries were packed; every charge was found proven. The law laid down a fine of £20 a month for not attending church – the Anglican church, that is – and the sessions of March 1682 fined 150 people. Soon after this, Hellier applied for writs against 500 non-attenders. Newgate was jammed with Dissenters who could not or would not pay the fine, and Hellier's squads had good exercise breaking into their shops and homes to seize goods which they sold for a fraction of their value. (On one occasion they ransacked a bedroom where the prisoner's wife was in child-bed.) By midsummer, 1,500 Dissenters were being prosecuted in one way or another, many dying in gaol, many released but reduced to beggary. In one year – 1683 – Bristol Quakers alone paid £16,440 in fines for non-attendance.

Hellier and Knight even attempted to revive an old and forgotten Act from Queen Elizabeth's days, which prescribed the death penalty for anyone who wouldn't conform to the Established Church. Hellier reached his zenith when he succeeded in getting one man, Richard Vickris, condemned to death under this Act, but the sentence was quashed on a technicality.

The hounding and bullying went on throughout 1684. When Charles II died and James II came to the throne in February 1685, Bristol's Newgate and Bridewell prisons held 120 Quakers who had been locked up for two years or more. Forbes, the minister of Broadmead Baptist chapel, had been inside for three years when he died in Gloucester gaol in November 1685.

Relief came with astonishing suddenness. In the spring of 1687, James II suspended all penal laws against Dissent, liberated those in gaol and declared that all sects were free to worship in public according to their faith. The fact that he did all this for the benefit of Roman Catholicism scarcely dampened the joy of the Dissenters.

For the first time, they were free under law. But as I said before, it's easier to change laws than people. In Bristol discrimination went on. The records of the Merchants Society (the Merchant Venturers) for 1711 show that Charles Harford, a merchant, applied to join and was rejected because he was a Quaker. Just to make its position quite clear, the Society passed a resolution: 'in future no professed Quaker should be admitted'. And three years later, a Bristol mob – hired and encouraged by a local group of fanatical Tories – celebrated the coronation of George I by attacking and looting Quakers' homes. When they reached the house of a man called Stephens, a Quaker friend tried to block the doorway. He was trampled to death. About ten rioters were arrested, tried, convicted, and sentenced – to three months' imprisonment, and a fine of £6 13s. 4d.

CHAPTER THREE

FIGHTING FITS

The Civil War between Charles I and Parliament was the biggest military operation this country experienced until 1914. Its outcome decided questions of enormous importance: whether or not the king's power was unlimited; whether or not Parliament could govern the country; whether or not freedom under law should be sacred.

The people of Bristol adopted a consistent attitude to this crucial struggle – consistently wishy-washy. Whenever possible they sat on the fence, bowing amiably in both directions. It is not surprising that they fell off, twice, and ended up very badly knocked about.

When the war began, early in 1642, Bristol was mildly in favour of Parliament without being firmly against the king. Charles had certainly behaved badly – his armed troopers had invaded the House of Commons, and Bristol paid for two M.P.s, remember – but that wasn't something Bristol was ready to go to war over, not with war the price it was. In April there were reports that some people in Redcliffe were organizing a rising; the sheriffs immediately raided the houses and seized a supply of clubs and other weapons. In May the Council appointed a committee to draft two petitions, one to be sent to Charles, the other to Parliament, urging a reconciliation. Bristol wanted the Civil War to go away.

It was all too late. After London, Bristol was the most important city in the land: a fortified seaport, a centre of great wealth. Both sides knew that the winner must have Bristol. Charles had already written to the mayor, ordering him to admit no troops and to defend Bristol for the royal cause. In June the Speaker of the House of Commons wrote asking Bristol to lend money to defend the kingdom; the Council lent £1,000 and the individual members raised a further £2,625. At the same time they answered Parliament's demand for two new M.P.s by sending up a pair of convinced royalists. Like the petitions of reconciliation, this was all part of the balancing act; and like the petitions (abandoned some months later because the drafting committee couldn't agree) it failed.

In July the Marquis of Hertford came west. Hertford was Lord Lieutenant of Somerset and Bristol, and Charles had sent him to make sure that both places were on his side. Bristol Council – anxious not to offend – got ready to receive him with all ceremony, but Hertford stayed at Wells instead, and sent a message asking permission to move his cavalry into Bristol. The mayor trotted out Charles' instructions not to admit anybody's troops. Hertford took the view that a city which was not for him must be against him, and he advanced.

He didn't get past Compton Mendip. The Somerset gentry were more Puritan and less pussyfooting than the men of Bristol. They intercepted the royalist column and scattered it after one brisk fight.

At last, Bristol stirred. The Corporation reluctantly recognized that there was a war on. Neutrality hadn't worked, but perhaps armed neutrality might, so they set about improving their defences. They repaired and strengthened the city walls and gates, mounted cannon and trained gunners, collected muskets and ammunition, bought a great deal of gunpowder and stockpiled food. If there had to be a siege maybe they could sit it out. Maybe they could sit out the whole war. Meanwhile, business went on. To finance its new defences the city had to borrow money, and alderman Gonning was pleased to lend £500 – at 7 per cent.

There was absolutely no sense of urgency. As usual, the Corporation gave itself a summer holiday, went duck-hunting, and fished in the Frome; in 1642 these outings lasted two days longer than usual. Parliament sent two Members to ask the Corporation for another loan; the Council turned them down. The Puritan gentry around Bristol formed an Association of Somerset, Gloucestershire and Wiltshire (ASGW) to defend the area against the king's armies; Bristol agreed to join, but did nothing about it.

The Corporation was not completely passive. Parliament had sent 2,000 soldiers to Bristol and the city agreed to pay for their victuals and to ship them to Ireland (where the fighting was heavier); but since Parliament was going to repay the city afterwards, this was not so much a generous gesture as a business deal. Besides, the city was probably glad to get rid of 2,000 restless soldiers.

On 23rd October the royal and parliamentary armies fought out a bloody draw at Edgehill, in Warwickshire. It was the first big battle of the war and it should have jolted Bristol into deciding who its friends were. The ASGW was getting annoyed at Bristol's sluggishness, and Alexander Popham – one of the leaders at Chewton Mendip – started planning to infiltrate his men into the city before the cavaliers could attack it. The mayor and aldermen tried to buy him with smiles. 'We shall be glad, when occasion shall require, to receive all friendly assistance from you,' they wrote, 'but as we now stand we conceive there is none.'

Popham disagreed. He warned Parliament that Bristol's inactivity threatened them all, and he asked for authority to lead 1,000 county troops into the city. Throughout this period the Corporation seems to have been incapable of doing anything decisive. On 8th November, according to the Council minutes, 'This day, the Mayor, Aldermen, Sheriffs and Common Council have declared themselves to be in love and amity one with another, and do desire a friendly association together in all things' – a sure sign that something disastrous was brewing. They revived the hopeless idea of appealing to king and Parliament to be reconciled, and again got nowhere with it. They sent representatives to meet the leaders of the ASGW at Bath, and the Bristol men waffled and havered so much that the county gentry lost patience. By now Parliament had authorized Popham's request. On 1st December, troops began moving into Bedminster and Westbury.

Right to the end, the Corporation wriggled and twisted to avoid having to take sides. On the one hand, they urged the ASGW to occupy Bristol quickly 'to avoid effusion of blood, which otherwise will doubtless happen', presumably from royalist resisters. On the other hand, they played out the charade of pretending to be reluctant to open the city's gates to Colonel Essex, who was bringing the main Roundhead garrison; it wasn't until the mayor's wife led a hundred female demonstrators into the council chamber that the city fathers allowed themselves to appear to be persuaded to hand the city over to Parliament. They had no choice, of course, but all the same they didn't want to seem too eager, just in case. When it came to taking sides, Bristol preferred the shuffle to the jump.

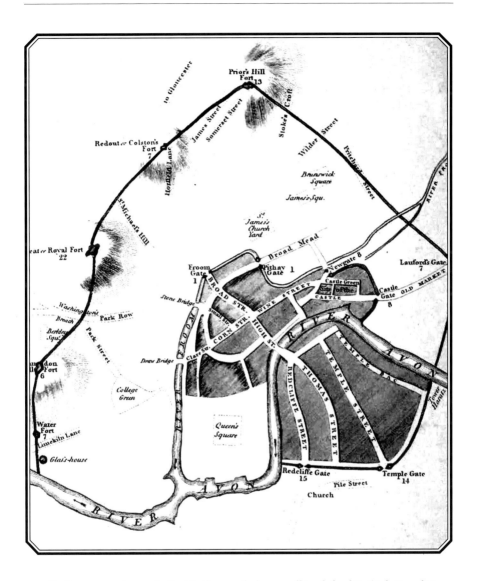

Parliamentary forces built this three-mile-long wall to defend Bristol. Royalist forces toiled for two years to strengthen it. Neither saved the city.

Essex arrived with 2,000 men. Now the war began to be expensive. In January 1643 Bristol lent £3,000 to the ASGW to raise an army and gave £3,400 to Essex for his garrison. A house-to-house collection had produced £2,600 for Parliament's war-fund, and, out in the fields to the north and west of the city, was being built the biggest expense of all: nearly three miles of fortified wall-and-ditch, running in a great loop from Tower Harritz (near what is now Temple Meads station) up through Stokes Croft, over Kingsdown and across Brandon Hill to rejoin the river. This massive job took three years to finish, and it just about bled Bristol white.

The obvious question is: why bother? Why go to all the effort of extending the area to be defended by three miles when there was a large and impressive castle sitting in the middle? The fact is that Bristol castle was impressive to the eye but vulnerable to the gun. It had been built to protect the city from attack by water, and cannon fire from the landward side would soon smash its elderly walls. Bristol, in fact, was a tricky place to hold.

A small army of labourers worked on the new defences all through that winter, throwing up the earth from the ditch to make a wall. From Tower Harritz to Lawford's Gate (at the east end of Old Market) and across to Stokes Croft the digging wasn't bad, but then they hit Kingsdown, St Michael's Hill, Brandon Hill: almost solid rock. The going was slow and costly. And there were three bastioned forts to be built, on Prior's Hill, Windmill Hill (now the Royal Fort) and Brandon Hill; as well as a few redoubts and lookouts and batteries. The cost must have been ferocious. Most of it probably came from the ratepayers, although the House of Commons also contributed, and the Corporation borrowed from all over, including the obliging alderman, Gonning, who this time provided £300 – at 8 per cent.

Colonel Essex had been made Governor of Bristol. The Puritans and the supporters of Parliament – probably three-quarters of the inhabitants – did not like him. He showed little enthusiasm for the fortifications, no interest in his men, and far too much liking for eating, drinking, gambling and 'keeping company of persons of known Royalist principles'. He was even rumoured to be in touch with Prince Rupert, who was the king's nephew and his best general. What was far worse, from the garrison's point of view, they hadn't been paid for several weeks, a situation which Bristol shopkeepers swiftly exploited by letting the soldiers buy on credit at vastly inflated prices.

It couldn't go on. About a month after their arrival in Bristol, twenty troopers and their captain went to see Essex.

It was not the best moment to see the Governor, because he was sleeping off a monumental debauch; but then, if they chose to wait for a moment when the Governor was neither drunk nor hung-over they might as well forget the whole thing. Essex was annoyed at being disturbed, and furious at being disturbed over something as trivial as soldiers' pay. He stamped into the room, waving a horse pistol, and ordered the troopers to get out. One man requested permission to speak. Essex shot him dead.

The next Governor was the Hon. Nathaniel Fiennes. He was a lawyer with little experience of soldiering, but he knew how to wake men up and get things done. The outer line of fortifications 'had more done unto them in five days than they had done unto them in six weeks before'. In his first three months in office he spent £9,000 on the works; then he got into his stride and by June he was laying out £1,000 a week – equivalent to at least £200,000 in modern money. The House of Commons sent him several thousand pounds, but heaven alone knows where he raised the rest; certainly not all in Bristol, which was already being taxed right, left and centre to support the garrison. Fiennes constantly appealed to Parliament for help. He complained that 'a false conceit was entertained of the riches of Bristol which, since the stop of trade and many malignants (i.e. Royalists) who drew in their estates, is much otherwise than is conceived by some'. Maybe – but there was still plenty of money to be taken out of Bristol by men who could squeeze harder than Fiennes.

By June 1643 Fiennes was so fed up that he asked to be relieved of his job; he said he hadn't half enough men to defend Bristol, and not enough money to support the men he had. Parliament turned down his request. Then something happened which underlined the urgent need for an outer wall – and demonstrated how incomplete the works still were.

Early in 1643 Prince Rupert had captured Cirencester. For a moment it looked like the start of something big, and in Gloucestershire and Bristol the royalists went around making loud and confident noises. The advance didn't work out, and Rupert had to pull his men back to Oxford, but nevertheless an attack on Bristol seemed a strong possibility.

Most of the royalist Bristolians were either merchants with happy memories of trading monopolies granted by the king, or Alf Garnetts. Robert Yeamans seems to have been a bit of both. He was a merchant and former sheriff, a man best described as 'one of those zealots whose rash enthusiasm is less dangerous to enemies than to friends'. Before the war, Charles I had given him a commission to raise a regiment in Bristol. On the strength of this, and a loud voice, he claimed the leadership of the local loyalists.

Yeamans was itching to see Prince Rupert in Bristol. He made friends with three disgruntled officers who said they thought Colonel Essex had had a raw deal. Yeamans told his royalist friends about this, and added that many troopers were also ready to defect. The civilians formed a confederacy, complete with an oath of loyalty and secrecy, which was administered by Yeamans' right-hand man, George Boucher, also a merchant.

The aim, of course, was to seize the city for the king. Yeamans sent his plan to Charles at Oxford; Charles vetted it, liked it, and approved it. He ordered Rupert to assist, and assured the confederates that they would be generously rewarded.

Yeamans chose the night of Tuesday 7th March.

His plan had the great virtue of simplicity. Thirty men, all armed, were to meet at his house in Wine Street; another sixty-odd would go to Boucher's house in Christmas Street. Two of the disgruntled officers would be on duty in the guard house, almost opposite Yeamans' place. At midnight, one officer would take a squad of soldiers and seize Frome Gate with the help of Boucher's men and two groups waiting in St Michael's parish. The other officer would surrender the guard house to Yeamans' men, who would use the cannon to clear the streets. Prince Rupert was waiting (ominously enough, beside the gallows on Cotham Hill) for the signals of success – the tolling of the bells of St Michael's and St John's and the blowing-up of a house. Everything was arranged: Yeamans had drawn up a proclamation; the plotters were to identify each other in the dark by wearing white tape on their hats; the password was *Charles*. It was not a very subtle password, but then it was not a very subtle plot. If all went well, shortly after midnight Prince Rupert would sweep down St Michael's Hill at the head of his men, gallop through Frome Gate and capture the city intact.

Fiennes knew the whole plot.

At 10 p.m. on the night, he called a council of war and sent two detachments of troops, one to Yeamans' house, one to Boucher's, with orders to arrest everyone there. He timed the raids perfectly. They were all inside.

When the soldiers beat on his door Yeamans refused to open up. They smashed their way in and a desperate fight surged through the house. Twenty-three men were caught; several escaped by scrambling over the roof. At Boucher's place there was less force and more farce. Many of the conspirators panicked and jumped out of a back window which overlooked the Frome. In one respect they were lucky: the tide was out. On the other hand the mud was deep, and they floundered helplessly and unhappily, for the Frome was notoriously an open sewer. Few got away.

Before dawn, the confederacy was in prison and Prince Rupert was on his way back to Oxford.

Noisy rejoicings followed. The salvation of Bristol confirmed the Parliamentary leaders' belief that the Almighty knew whose side He was on. 'And so God put a hook in their nostrils', crowed a Bristol preacher during the national Thanksgiving. God was not infallible – a gang of conspirators hijacked two ships and got clean away – but still, three days after the event Fiennes had about 60 men chained by neck and foot inside the castle, where they had leisure to hold their gloomy post-mortems.

Where had they gone wrong? The big failure had been security. As many as 200 people were in the plot; as many as 2,000 knew about it. Inevitably, something leaked. Yeamans didn't exactly encourage total secrecy: his unofficial 'party headquarters' was the

Rose tavern, and he was a man who enjoyed talking. The heavy hints dropped like bricks. There was a credible rumour that 'a plot was discovered by some tattling females who were acting on the Parliament's side the night before': the old, old story of men shooting off their mouths in a whorehouse. Above all, there was the dangerous ease with which Yeamans recruited those three garrison officers. Treachery like theirs deserved an automatic death-sentence; instead, no record of any punishment exists. They were almost certainly feeding Yeamans' plans straight back to Fiennes. If so, the coup never stood a chance.

Now came the reckoning. Most of the prisoners were allowed to ransom themselves by forfeiting their estates. Only four went to trial: Yeamans and his brother William; Boucher; and a plumber called Edward Dacres. All were condemned to death, but William Yeamans and Dacre were reprieved. The king tried to save Robert Yeamans and Boucher by threatening to kill some of the Roundheads captured at Cirencester, as a reprisal; it was only a gesture and it failed. A pair of Puritan preachers – Cradock and Fowler; they even *sound* like Puritans – harangued the two men in their cells and got absolutely no change out of them; they stuck to their principles. On 30th May 1643, outside the Nag's Head in Wine Street, Yeamans and Boucher were hanged, drawn and quartered. They left a total of sixteen children and – what was worse for Bristol – a great deal of royalist bitterness.

The Yeamans-Boucher plot should have taught Bristol one thing: that the outer wall wasn't much of an obstacle. It certainly hadn't worried Rupert. Yet the Corporation remained cheerfully complacent. The fortifications 'were in great forwardness', they told the House of Commons in May. That depended on where you stood and how you looked. Certainly a lot had been done: forts were standing on Brandon Hill, Windmill Hill, Prior's Hill; guns had also been mounted in Tower Harritz and Water Fort, guarding the ends of the wall, as well as at Lawford's Gate and Temple Gate. But what about the bits *between* the forts? Down in the low ground the rampart looked good. Up on the hill they were still hacking out the rock.

Charles I: God made him king, but nobody could make him a great general. His army taxed Bristol until it was bankrupt: bad tactics.

It was no time to take chances, which is exactly what Parliament did. Sir William Waller withdrew troops from the Bristol garrison to strengthen his army. On 5th July he fought the Royalists at Lansdown, failed to win, challenged them again a week later at Roundway in Wiltshire, and was smashed to pieces. Bang went the last Parliamentary army in the west.

The king's next move was obvious.

Although Fiennes had only 2,000 infantry and 300 cavalry to defend Bristol against Prince Rupert's army of 20,000, he announced that he was determined to hold out to the end. By Saturday 22nd July, Rupert's men were all around the city. Next day the Prince went to afternoon service in Clifton church. On Monday the siege began.

It says a lot for Fiennes' work that the first day's attacks got nowhere. Rupert tried harder on Tuesday, with the same result. In the evening he called his officers together and planned a dawn attack: first a cannonade, and then the simultaneous storming of six separate points.

Came the dawn, and once again the defences held firm. On the Redcliffe side of the city Lord Hertford's Cornish regiments charged the ancient, massive ramparts and 'were repelled with great slaughter'. Lord Grandison led an assault on Prior's Hill Fort (commanding the eastern end of Kingsdown) and was beaten off. All the other attacks fizzled out. The cavaliers never enjoyed sieges, and this one was becoming discouraging. By breakfast-time the Cornishmen had given up and were walking home, when unexpectedly the whole picture changed.

Rupert had reconnoitred the wall and found it 'but indifferently fortified', yet he had failed to spot its weakest point.

Between Brandon Hill Fort and Windmill Fort – the place which is now Queens Road, by the museum – lay a hollow. *Here the rampart had never been finished.* If Fiennes expected the forts to cover the gap with their cannon he was mistaken, because the guns couldn't be aimed low enough to fire into the hollow. What's more, thick furze and undergrowth on the slopes helped to mask an attack.

Luckily for Rupert he had ordered Captain Washington (ancestor of the great American) to threaten this point as a diversion; and luckily again, Washington knew a half-open door when he saw one. He led a 'fire-pike' charge – pikemen with bundles of blazing straw tied to their weapons – and rapidly routed the defenders. At once he sent for reinforcements while his men shovelled the earthwork into the ditch. The royalist cavalry galloped through the gap. By 9 a.m. they were at the cathedral. Fiennes ordered a counter-attack on College Green, but his men were exhausted after four days' continuous duty. Only 200 made the attempt; they failed. Rupert pressed on through the narrow, twisting streets – one report says he lost 'five hundred men, who were shot by the inhabitants from the walls and windows' – and stormed Frome Gate. The defenders fought stubbornly, and there was no lack of arms and ammunition. Suddenly Fiennes gave in.

Technically, it was not yet a surrender, only a parley; but once Fiennes halted the defence he could never hope to restart it. Rupert was surprised and delighted (as were the Cornishmen, some of whom had got as far as Whitchurch). He and Fiennes met in a garden near Park Row and agreed on terms. The treaty of surrender was signed that evening. Bristol was in royal hands.

For the second time that year, the deliverance of the city was the cause of a national thanksgiving. Charles ordered this one. The capture of Bristol boosted his prospects higher than ever before: now he controlled nearly all the west, and he threatened everything he didn't control. His men set it to verse:

> *Bristol taking,*
> *Exeter shaking,*
> *Glocester quaking*

and that was a fair summary of the situation. The cavaliers were entitled to boast; they had no right to gloat. The surrender treaty was fair and honourable, and they broke it like a cracked cup.

The terms of this treaty allowed all the Parliamentary forces, with their arms and horses, their sick and wounded, to be escorted to Warminster. In Bristol, civilians' rights and property were to be respected, and the liberties of the city maintained. The opposite happened. Eight hundred of Fiennes' troops – and Fiennes himself – were insulted, ill treated, robbed, beaten and in some cases stripped almost naked; then they were thrown out. Rupert's men treated Bristol like one big grab bag: anything they wanted they took. They looted homes, plundered shops, evicted families to make room for billets. The Corporation, shocked by the pillage, offered Rupert £1,400 to call off his men. He took the money. The violence went on. Rupert had little interest in anybody's rights or privileges except his own and the king's; and besides, Bristol was being made to pay for Yeamans and Boucher.

Fiennes went to London to face the music. Parliament was in a rage: hadn't he spent all that money on ramparts, and promised to fight to the end? A council of war convicted him of cowardice and sentenced him to death; but later Cromwell pardoned him. Cromwell himself said that Fiennes was right to surrender when further resistance was useless. He could have retreated into the castle for a last stand, but in that case Rupert would probably have burned the rest of Bristol. Fiennes had the civilians to think of: the rules of war allowed a besieger to wipe out the inhabitants when a city refused to surrender after there was no longer any reasonable hope of winning. Even before the parley, Fiennes' troops had begun to desert (1,000 stayed on to do garrison-duty for Rupert) and the royalists were blockading the mouth of the Avon. Above all, that lengthy perimeter had proved to be as much of a weakness as a strength. Fiennes had to try and spread his men along four miles of wall (including the Redcliffe ramparts) – yet one hole punched in that wall had let Rupert's army pour through like sand through a funnel. After that breach, the wall was irrelevant. Rupert got much glory from his capture of Bristol; before long he was to discover just how hard Fiennes' job had been.

And before long, Bristolians were to discover just how greedy the military appetite can be. They had complained about Parliament's demands for money and protested their desperate poverty; now the royalists – who saw no need to be sweet and reasonable –

proceeded to milk Bristol dry. Then they kicked it in the ribs and milked it again. In 1643 the citizens still had plenty of cash sewn into their mattresses for a rainy day. The king had a lot of bad weather ahead of him.

When their £1,400 sweetener failed, the Council offered Charles a gift of £10,000 in token of the 'love and good affection' of the city. Charles was not impressed. Most of the money was raised by a rate on householders; the looting went on, so the householders paid twice over. In October the Council – desperate now – raised £20,000 for Charles and Rupert: a colossal amount to collect from only 15,000 people when you remember that trade was bad and the people were already paying a weekly levy of £400 to support the garrison.

The Corporation had a touching faith in gifts of wine. When Charles came to Bristol in August and appointed Rupert as Governor, they presented the Prince with a butt and three hogsheads of wine and a hundredweight of sugar. They also gave him the freedom of the city, which was like saying grace to a well-fed tiger. When Charles returned to Oxford he got regular offerings of wine, which he took, together with humble petitions, which he ignored. In February 1644 he finally consented to grant Bristol his gracious pardon for having opposed him and hanged his two 'martyrs', but the document cost the city £150, plus gifts, and it made precious little difference to the way he shoved the Corporation around – expelling councillors he didn't like and demanding that keen royalists be made mayor and sheriffs. To him, Bristol was an ex-Roundhead city that had proclaimed its loyalty with suspicious speed and fervour. It was to be trusted to the minimum and exploited to the maximum. By May 1644 Bristolians were paying a huge rate, levied every week, to finance stronger fortifications, *plus* extra taxes to finish the new Royal Fort, *plus* contributions towards a lump sum of £2,000 for the garrison. On top of all that, the 'mock' Parliament set up by Charles at Oxford had voted him £100,000, and Bristol's share came from – where else? – the ratepayers. Bristol's M.P. at Oxford was alderman Taylor. Until Fiennes surrendered, Taylor had been

Prince Rupert, the king's nephew, promised to hold Bristol for three months, and then tamely surrendered after 18 days. His uncle said his judgement had been 'seduced by some rotten-hearted villains'.

Bristol's M.P. at Westminster. No wonder Charles looked sideways at Bristol.

His men held Bristol for two years, and for two years Bristol paid and paid and paid, until the Corporation was bankrupt and the city was beggared. Already, when Rupert took over, there was such a chronic shortage of cash that a mint was set up to convert silver plate into coin – halfcrowns, shillings, sixpences – and gold into sovereigns and half-sovereigns. Even this wasn't enough: the king's soldiers had to be paid in 'Bristol farthings', tokens stamped out of base metal. There was a savage touch of Catch-22 about Bristol's position: the worse the war went for Charles, the more demands he made on the city and the harder it was to meet them – because the war itself was costing Bristol more and more. For instance, early in 1644 Roundhead ships had become such a menace in the Bristol Channel that the Corporation and the Governor of Chepstow agreed to split the cost of keeping a pinnace on patrol. So many Bristol merchantmen were taken by the Puritan navy that a second pinnace had to be sent out. Chepstow never paid its share of either boat. Bristol threatened to withdraw the patrols. Charles wouldn't allow it. And *still* ships were lost; so many, in fact, that Bristol merchants had to send their goods by Dutch vessels – or not at all.

The royalist demands were never-ending. By the spring of 1644 it was costing about £2,000 a week to strengthen the city's defences, maintain the garrison (3,600 foot-soldiers, 420 cavalry, the Prince's own troop of 200, and 60 gunners) and manufacture arms and ammunition. Bristol's share was only £150 – the rest came from the neighbouring counties – but the ratepayers also had to scrape together £1,000 a year for the relief of maimed soldiers.

In April, Queen Henrietta Maria slept here. The Corporation had a struggle to make her comfortable (the landlord of the Red Lion ended up lending some beds) and when they decided to give her £500 'as a token of their love', mostly by levying an extra rate, their love fell about £40 short. Next month the Council borrowed £1,000 to expand the Trained Band; eventually this bill too came back to the ratepayer.

The news from the battlefield was not encouraging, either.

Rupert's army took a pasting at Marston Moor on 2nd July. He came back to a Bristol whose treasury was empty and whose credit was low. The Corporation managed to borrow £200 to finish the Royal Fort and another £200 towards the cost of entertaining Rupert, but when the royalists wanted £160 to pay for their warships on the Severn, Bristol could find only £20. Rupert demanded yet more money for siege preparations, so the Council doubled the garrison levy on householders, then doubled it again when the king required 1,500 pairs of shoes and stockings for his army. In October Charles thought it would be a good idea if Bristol helped Somerset to raise a new army. Lord Hopton, the Lieutenant-Governor, suggested £2,000 in cash and £1,000 in kind. The Council nearly fainted. It took them two days to find the strength for a reply: they voted to *lend* the king only £1,000; and when he demanded another £1,500 they told him (with refreshing frankness) that it simply wasn't possible. The fact was that Bristol was getting groggy at the knees. The great St James' Fair hadn't been held that year, many houses were standing empty because the tenants had fled, and inland trade had just about collapsed.

By March 1645, when the fifteen-year-old Prince of Wales came to Bristol, things were looking desperate. The Corporation was so hard up that it had to borrow furniture, beds and bedding for the mini-Court, and the Prince had to eat his royal breakfast off common pewter. The Council generously voted to present him with £500 as a gift from his loyal ratepayers; this time loyalty stopped short at £430. The bucket had been to the well too often. In April the Corporation – under protest – sent its collectors out to raise an extra £400 which the Prince's Council needed to pay for provisioning the castle and the Royal Fort; but it looks as if they drew a blank, because on 15th May the Prince suggested that the aldermen might *lend* him £400 and take it out of the arrears. The aldermen declined. Double-blank.

In any case, they had graver problems: the plague was upon Bristol. It struck in April and raged for seven months. The Council set up a pest house where the victims could be isolated, and borrowed money to help relieve their suffering. (A £100 loan from alderman Farmer was repaid *thirteen* years later: a measure of how utterly the war had exhausted Bristol.) Nobody kept a total of deaths, but the plague killed 32 people in the last week of October alone, when it was supposedly almost over. The death roll probably reached 3,000: one-fifth of the population.

All this time the royalists had been raising and strengthening the outer defences which Fiennes had left them. If a household couldn't pay its share – in advance – then it had to send a man to work on the wall: 6 a.m. to 6 p.m., with a two-hour break at midday. Even so, Bristol couldn't supply enough manpower. Rupert's men went into Somerset and Gloucestershire, conscripted labourers, and levied the workers' pay from whichever district had provided them.

Rupert kept this labour-force at work for nearly two years, strengthening the ramparts – he made sure that Washington's Breach had a hefty wall built across it – and improving the forts. The biggest job was converting Windmill Fort to Royal Fort, a great five-sided citadel with 22 guns, a magazine and a barracks. All the forts which studded the wall were now formidably armed: Colston's Redoubt and Prior's Hill Fort on Kingsdown had seven and thirteen guns respectively. In all, 140 cannon defended Bristol.

The battle of Naseby on 14th June 1645 made a second siege of Bristol inevitable. Rupert's defeat in the field meant that he would have to try and fight the war from his strongholds. By 12th August he was assuring Charles that he would hold Bristol for at least three months. Certainly he was far better placed than Fiennes had been. Rupert had his expert staff and a garrison of 4,000 with ample munitions, and for months they had been stockpiling food (including 12,000 gallons of beer).

He hadn't long to wait. Sir Thomas Fairfax led the Roundhead army in a rapid mopping-up of the west. He scattered the royalists at Langport on 10th July, took Bridgwater on the 21st, Bath on the 29th, and Sherborne Castle on 15th August. That left Bristol. Five days later Fairfax and his Lieutenant-General, Cromwell, reached

Chew Magna. The Cavaliers were out burning villages so that the enemy would have no shelter from the rain; Bedminster, Clifton and part of Westbury went up in flames, but the Roundheads saved Keynsham, Hanham and Stapleton. They also amazed and delighted the locals by paying in cash for all their needs, which made a nice change after the thud-and-plunder of the Cavaliers.

Fairfax spent a couple of days looking at the defences and getting his army in place. Then on 23rd August the siege began, in steady rain. A battery on Ashley Down hurled cannonballs at Royal Fort and Prior's Hill Fort. Rupert – temperamentally unsuited to a war of waiting – sent his cavalry out of Royal Fort looking for trouble, but the Roundheads beat them off. That was the pattern for the next three days: Roundhead pressure, a Cavalier sally, no success either way, continuous rain. On the 27th, Portishead Point surrendered and five Parliamentary warships blockaded the Avon. The 28th was quiet, the 29th saw yet another royalist sally come to nothing, and on 1st September Rupert made his biggest effort yet. A thousand cavalry and six hundred foot charged out of Royal Fort. They blundered about in the rain and mist, killed one Roundhead officer, captured another, and retired. Clearly Rupert was not going to raise this siege by fighting off his besiegers.

On the other hand the Roundheads weren't getting very far either. It was already September; the weather was soggy; in those days armies usually packed up campaigning in October, and a rumour said the king was moving westward to relieve Bristol. On 2nd September Fairfax held a council of war. The Roundhead leaders decided to take the city by storm.

By 4th September the weather was clearing and they were ready to attack. Fairfax appealed to Rupert to surrender and avoid bloodshed. Rupert stalled: he asked for time to contact Charles, asked to discuss terms, and asked for the terms to be put in writing. Fairfax decided that Rupert was stringing him along. On Wednesday 10th September he gave orders for the storm to begin at two o'clock the following morning.

His plan of attack was similar to Rupert's: a simultaneous assault at several different points. The ramparts were much stronger than in 1643, and so the storm was spearheaded by squads of 200 picked men – known rather discouragingly as 'forlorn hopes' – who would get, if they survived, an extra twenty shillings. The first rank of 40 forlorn hopes carried 20 ladders; then came musketeers, under a sergeant; then five files of armed men led by a lieutenant; finally seven files commanded by a captain. This order of battle was based on the assumption that the first men to reach the wall would die: a ladder-carrier wasn't worth a musket; a sergeant was more expendable than a lieutenant, a lieutenant less valuable than a captain. If the forlorn hopes could break (or dent) the defences, 200 more men charged; after them came the 'pioneers' to rip down the wall and clear a breach for the cavalry.

At 2 a.m. the battery on Ashley Down boomed out a salvo and a huge heap of straw was fired: the signals to attack. Four regiments of infantry faced the southern ramparts which curved through Redcliffe. This was where the Cornish royalists had taken such a beating; now the Roundheads failed just as completely. No fewer than three separate assaults by forlorn hopes were shot to pieces. As a survivor put it: 'the works on that side were so high that the ladders could not near reach them'. Some Roundhead officer had failed to do his homework properly.

On the northern side, the crucial target was considered to be Prior's Hill Fort. Three regiments were concentrated on it; but once again the scaling ladders were too short: thirty rungs barely reached the parapet. It was an extraordinarily elementary blunder, considering that the Roundheads had had a week to get ready. It cost them dear, because the Cavaliers let fly with cannon and musket and simply blasted the enemy off the face of the fort. Not surprisingly, the assault on Royal Fort also got precisely nowhere.

All this was desperate stuff, but it makes you wonder why they chose to attack the forts at all, when they could have gone over the wall between them. Washington had shown the quickest way to get into Bristol, and, even after all the royalist building, the northern rampart reached no great height – probably five feet at the most. Rupert himself said that 'the breast-work (was) low and thin, the graff (ditch) narrow and of no depth, and by the opinion of all the colonels, not tenable on a brisk and vigorous assault'. Presumably the Roundheads, like the Cavaliers before them, felt that the soldierly thing to do was to challenge the enemy at his strongest point – a piece of military vanity which persisted as late as 1944, when the American forces on D-Day chose to hit the beach *opposite* the German bunkers rather than between them.

Luckily for Fairfax, the brigade ordered to attack Lawford's Gate got over the rampart nearby and was able to storm the position from all sides. They opened the gate to the cavalry, which took Old Market at the gallop and forced the great gate of the castle. At about the same time the sallyport at Stokes Croft was captured, and at length a Roundhead force fought its way up the hill inside the wall until it could take Prior's Hill Fort from the rear. By then the royalists had fought off nearly three hours of frontal attacks, and their opponents were grim with rage. When the Roundheads got inside and started hacking, very few defenders were allowed to surrender.

Fairfax had the breakthrough he needed. One big reason for his success was his decision to make a night attack. This was ungentlemanly, and not the Cavaliers' way of fighting, because it meant that the guns of the various forts couldn't see to cover each other. By day, Prior's Hill Fort was in full view of Royal Fort and the castle – a fact which was brought home to Fairfax and Cromwell shortly after dawn. They were standing on the parapet, taking a look at the city below, when a cannon shot from the castle missed them by six inches. If that royalist gunner had nudged his muzzle by just a hairsbreadth, the history of England might have been very different.

Rupert was far from beaten. He still held four powerful forts and most of the castle, plus all the southern ramparts; and his men had enough stores to hold out for weeks. Yet soon after daybreak royalist morale was so bad that they were setting fire to parts of the town. By mid-morning Rupert had lost his nerve and proposed a surrender. After all his big battles and his big talk, it was a startling collapse.

Rupert himself claimed that he had fewer than 1,500 men to

defend his lines, that 'many of those were new levied Welch', and that 'it was impossible to keep them from getting over the works' – and, presumably, deserting. But there seems to have been another, more sinister, reason why he gave in.

Months later, Charles I said of Rupert's surrender that 'this great error proceeded not from change of affection, but by having his judgement seduced by some rotten-hearted villains'. We can put a name to one villain: alderman Hooke, mayor of Bristol the previous year and an oily opportunist who changed his loyalties as often as he changed his underwear – or possibly more often, 17th-century hygiene being what it was.

Hooke had something on Rupert. Whether it was blackmail, or bribery, or sheer bluff, nobody ever found out, but it was powerful enough for Rupert to send his commissioners scrambling out under a white flag to start a parley. Five years later, when Hooke was in some legal trouble and Cromwell got him out of it, Cromwell justified this by saying that Hooke had done 'something considerable' to help the Puritans which was 'for many reasons desired to be concealed'. While the king held Bristol, Hooke had paraded as a red-hot royalist, which may have given him the opportunity to prepare some massive piece of treachery. Whatever it was, it brought the siege to a sharp halt.

Fairfax treated Rupert a damn sight better than Rupert had treated Fiennes. The royalists were allowed to ride out with their arms and baggage and a Roundhead escort to protect them from the furious peasantry who were out in force to see them off – with clubs. Fairfax and Cromwell moved into Bristol and found a disaster area. 'It looked more like a prison than a city,' reported a visitor, 'the people ... brought so low with taxations, so poor in habit, and so dejected in countenance; the streets so noisome, and the houses so nasty ... they were unfit to receive friends till they were cleansed.'

The Corporation's footwork was getting nimbler with practice, and in no time at all the Council was staunchly Roundhead in politics. To underline their reliability they gave Fairfax two pipes of wine (210 gallons), and when Colonel Skipton was made

*Cromwell was on the Kingsdown heights, watching the
Roundhead assault on Bristol, when a Royalist cannon-shot
missed him by six inches. Sometimes luck makes history.*

Governor they gave him a pipe of canary and two hogsheads of
claret. They also raised – God knows how – a £6,000 'gratuity' to
keep the soldiers happy.

It all sounds depressingly familiar. Slice it where you like, the
city's record in the Civil War was nothing to be proud of. Most
Bristolians simply looked after their own interests 'by favouring
whichever party got uppermost, and by deserting each in turn
when the tide of fortune turned'.

Even after Parliament had recaptured Bristol, the Corporation
kept an eye on the chances of a royal come-back. In March 1646
the Chamberlain laid out 3s. 6d. 'for wood for the bonfire before
Mr Mayor's door on Coronation Day, being the King's Holiday'.
The same anniversary was observed in 1647, and again in 1648. In
1649 Charles was beheaded, and the bonfires stopped. When there
was only one side left, Bristol knew which side it was on.

CHAPTER FOUR

BLACK SLAVERY

There was never a negro slave-market in Bristol. The idea that shiploads of African slaves were auctioned on Blackboy Hill is a myth – a hardwearing and well-beloved myth, but obviously bogus: why bring great numbers of slaves to Bristol when their destination is America or the West Indies? It is strange that Bristolians should choose to stain the record unnecessarily, when Bristol's involvement in black slavery was already about as horrible as it could be.

Between 1698 (when London's monopoly of slave-trading was broken) and 1807 (when Parliament abolished the trade), English ships carried at least 7,000,000, and perhaps as many as 10,000,000, African slaves across the Atlantic. No accurate record was kept, but we know that the total for one year, 1788, was 74,000, and this was long after the trade had passed its peak. Nobody kept count of the death rate at sea either, but it was commonplace for a slave-ship to lose a quarter of her cargo before she reached port, and many of the slaves she unloaded died soon after. If we count only the slaves who died at sea, it follows that, in all, something like two million black corpses were thrown overboard by English slavers. This was the trade which the Corporation of Bristol and the Society of Merchant Venturers warmly endorsed as 'the great support of our people at home, and the foundation of our trade abroad'.

And they were absolutely correct – economically speaking. Bristol made a fortune out of slavery; it was the eighteenth century's equivalent of a licence to print money. The instant London lost its monopoly, Bristol jumped in. By 1709, 57 slave ships were sailing from Bristol; 20 years later the number was up to 80 or 90. In the 1750s Bristol may even have passed London and become the chief slaving port – by 1755 no fewer than 155 Bristol merchants were trading in slaves – although Liverpool, too, was coming up fast.

The fascination of slaving was its triple profit. The ships sailed a triangular route: from Bristol to West Africa with a cargo of stuff like brassware, cotton, gin, muskets, which were sold or bartered for slaves and ivory, at a profit; then the 'Middle Passage' from West Africa to the American or West Indian colonies, where the slaves were sold, at a profit; and then home to Bristol with a hold full of molasses or tobacco and ivory, which brought a final and handsome profit. The slave trade was a huge, roaring bandwagon and all the city fathers were on board: mayors, sheriffs, aldermen, councillors, Merchant Venturers, and last but not least Mr Edward Colston, M.P., who shrewdly invested much of his considerable wealth in the slave trade and got it all back again umpteen times over, a feat which the boys and girls of Colston's Schools might ponder as they kneel in prayer on Founder's Day.

A man could retire in luxury on the profits from a good slaving trip. The voyage of the *Dispatch* was typical. She sailed from Bristol in October 1725 with a cargo of firearms, cotton goods, metal bars, copper pans, hats and so on. Total value: £1,330. Trading this for 240 choice slaves and ivory and then selling the slaves to plantation-owners for £13 10s. each brought in £3,240 – with the profit on sugar and ivory still to come.

Or take the *Freke Galley*, owned by William Freke & Co. of Bristol, which carried 329 slaves to Barbados in 1730. Although the 141 men, 75 women, 65 boys and 48 girls were listed as 'not all in good condition', they fetched £6,207. A good voyage with about 270 healthy slaves usually made a total profit of £7,000 or more. In 1755 the *Pearl* of Bristol sold her slaves in South Carolina for almost £8,000.

Pickings like these attracted plenty of competition, and in the 1720s at least 30,000 Africans a year were being shipped to the West Indies alone. Yet the price which plantation-owners paid steadily went up. From £13 10s. per slave in 1725 it rose to about £30 in 1760, as much as £60 in 1774, and in the 1790s settled at around £50 per adult and £40 per child.

There were two reasons for this increase.

In the first place, it was getting harder to catch Africans on the Slave Coast; the trade had nearly emptied the area. Between 1700 and 1750, 408,101 slaves were shipped from West Africa to Jamaica *alone*. Of these, 108,000 got transferred to other islands, which still left a net gain of 300,000. Yet – and this is the second reason – there was so much sickness and death on Jamaica that by 1750 the gain on paper of 300,000 had been turned into a loss of *more* than 300,000: the population figures showed scarcely any natural growth at all since 1700. In 1774 Jamaica needed six thousand new slaves a year simply to keep its workforce up to strength.

And slaves were an unusual commodity, often hard to come by. The standard technique was to let *other* Africans do the actual slave-raiding and then buy from them. After a war between the tribes, slaves were plentiful, which was why Bristol merchants made a point of sending plenty of firearms, ammunition and gin to the Slave Coast. The trouble with letting the natives do it was that sometimes they brought back the wrong sort of slave – too young or too old, not strong enough or an unpopular colour – so the slave-ships used to send white men to help direct operations.

As the areas near the coast were stripped bare, so the slaving expeditions had to go deeper and deeper inland to find a native village or camp. Usually they attacked at night. There would be a few minutes of screaming, shrieking panic and chaos; perhaps some resistance, ruthlessly cut down; a desperate scramble to grab the escapers; and when dawn came up another parcel of slaves was waiting, clubbed into submissiveness and roped together for the long forced march to the sea.

On the way they passed the bleached bones of victims of earlier marches. Nowadays this image has become a cinema cliché; like all good clichés it has a hard core of truth. Most slave-raids left a few bodies lying beside the track before they got to the coast. From the slavers' point of view this was no real loss: if a captive couldn't survive the march, he certainly wouldn't survive the voyage. Physical fitness was the only thing they were interested in. They took children and left parents who were too old, took parents and left children who were too young. They separated husbands from wives, brusquely, clinically, permanently. The slaves who reached the coast were utterly wretched. Then they saw the ocean, and that completed their ordeal.

These were *inland* tribesmen; they had never seen the sea before. Most of them had probably never even heard of it. The thing looked sickeningly big and full of menace. The news that they were going to be sent on it, far away, altogether out of sight of land for weeks on end, frightened them to an extent which we can hardly imagine. There were other horrors before they sailed – they were driven like cattle to the slave-market, examined like cattle, bought like cattle and, like cattle, branded with a hot iron – but their greatest suffering came when they were forced on board. The idea of going inside those stinking, sweltering ships terrified the Africans so much that suicide was a real problem to the owners. In 1725 Isaac Hobhouse & Co. Ltd. of Bristol instructed one of their masters:

'So soon as you begin to slave, let the netting be fixed breast high fore and aft, and so keep them shackled and hand-bolted to prevent their rising or leaping overboard.'

On Bristol ships it was customary to chain the bigger slaves by the neck; nevertheless the Middle Passage was a long trip and sometimes the slaves saw their chance to end their misery in the deep blue sea. This happened on the Bristol ship *Princess of Orange* in 1737, as the captain reported:

'... a 100 of men slaves jumped overboard, and it was with great difficulty we saved as many as we did. We lost 33 ... who were resolved to die. Some others have died since, but not to the owner's loss, they being sold before any discovery was made of the injury the salt water had done them.'

To understand the desperation which drove the negroes to drown themselves, you first have to appreciate the nightmarish conditions in which they lived.

Bristol slave-ships were not big. A typical vessel was the 100-ton *Williamsburg*, which carried 335 slaves. (By contrast, the *Mayflower* of 180 tons carried only 102 pilgrims.) To stow 335 living bodies meant packing every inch. The hold was about five feet high, so the owners had added a six-foot-wide platform halfway up, on both sides of the ship. The slaves were driven into the hold and forced to lie on the bottom, in rows, until it was covered; then

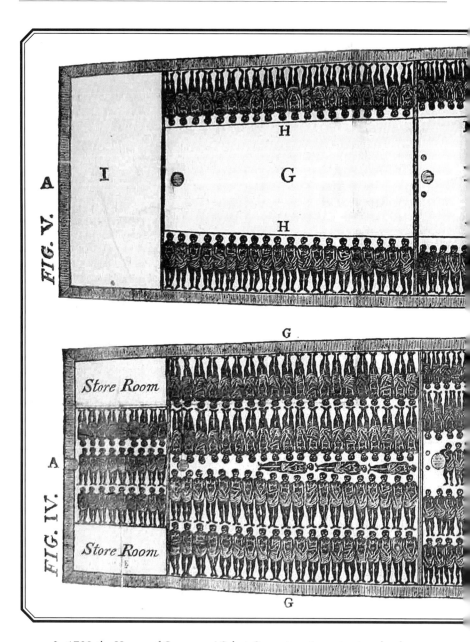

*In 1788 the House of Commons' Select Committee investigating the slave
trade sent a naval captain to measure the slaveship Brookes, 320 tons,
and calculate her legal cargo. His plans show how 451 slaves could*

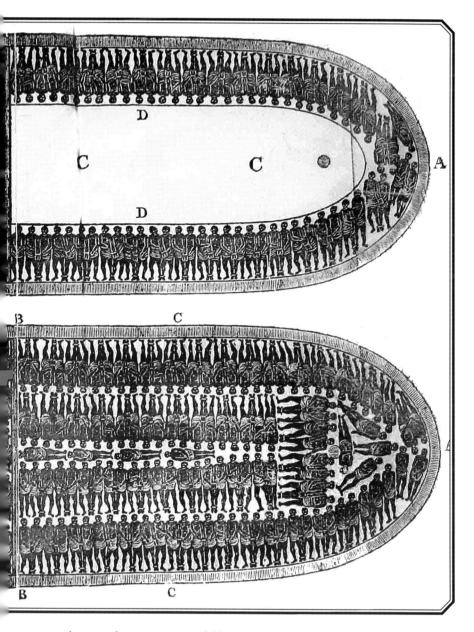

be stowed, using every available space until the bodies touched. In fact the ship's legal maximum was 454, but he could find no space to draw the other three. On one voyage the Brookes had carried 600 slaves.

another layer of slaves was packed in rows along the platforms. (In slightly larger ships a second platform was sometimes installed, leaving only 20 inches of headroom for each of the three layers of slaves.)

To get them all in, the stowing had to be scientific: the tallest men were put amidships; the smaller ones and the children were wedged into the stern. Finally the bodies touched each other and there was only room for them to sleep on their sides, 'spoon fashion'. The space was all carefully worked out: for a male slave – 6 feet by 16 inches; a female slave – 5 feet by 16 inches; a boy slave – 5 feet by 14 inches; a girl slave – 4 feet 6 inches by 12 inches. In those spaces they had to live for weeks. They were seasick, there were no lavatories, and those who were chained had no choice but to foul themselves. Add the tropical heat, the bad food, the shortage of water and the absence of ventilation, and you have a formula for human degradation comparable with the camps of Belsen and Buchenwald.

And this was not the worst. When business was brisk, the slavers took all the cargo they could get on board. Although she was only 90 tons, the *Tryal* of Bristol carried 356 slaves on one voyage and 390 on another. The *Bryce* of Bristol was only 100 tons, but somehow her captain jammed 414 slaves into her holds. At the other extreme were ships like a little 11-ton Bristol slaver with a space between decks only 32 inches high; thirty slaves were packed in there, unable to sit upright or stretch at full length.

Many died. On 4th November 1729, the *John & Betty* of Bristol reached Jamaica with 150 slaves; a hundred had died during the passage; eleven more died when they got ashore. In the same year the galley *Greyhound* – one of Isaac Hobhouse's ships – left West Africa with 339 slaves and landed only 214 at Barbados. Some died from exhaustion, some from sickness, some because they wanted to die. With so much human flesh crammed into so small a space, pestilence was always a threat, and when it broke out nobody was safe. In 1764 the *St Michael* of Bristol reached St Christopher in the West Indies after a voyage during which disease had killed 200 slaves – plus 12 crew and the captain. Two years earlier, the cargo of the *Defence,* another Bristol slaver, had fared even worse. When she foundered off the African coast only the captain and crew were saved. Four hundred and sixty slaves drowned.

Ship-owners insured negroes just as they insured other cargoes, and the records of Bristol firms are full of arguments with their brokers over things like whether or not certain negroes died of natural causes. In 1785 one of these disputes ended up in court, in front of Lord Mansfield. During the Middle Passage, the cargo of 225 slaves had twice 'mutinied' (that was the owner's word, reproachfully). In the fighting, 19 had been killed on board and 36 had died after jumping over the side and swallowing seawater. The shippers claimed compensation for all 55. The underwriters maintained that they were liable only for the 19. Mansfield ruled in favour of the underwriters, pointing out that the 36 had not died as a direct result of the mutiny, and that this particular insurance didn't cover everyday wastage such as damage from salt water.

Other insurance policies operated the other way round. There is a record of a long, slow voyage to Jamaica during which sickness broke out, more than 60 negroes died and the rest were so racked with dysentery that the captain began to doubt whether they would fetch any price at all; what's more the water supply was very low. The captain called the officers together and explained his dilemma. If any more slaves died of sickness or thirst the loss would fall on the owners, but if they were dumped in the sea this would be a legal jettison, which was covered by insurance. We can probably guess their decision. It's much harder to understand the mentality which allows a man to drown a hundred or more slaves, but won't let him do anything so dishonourable as tell a lie to an insurance company.

For 70 or 80 slaves to die on the Middle Passage was quite normal. Nevertheless, the captains of the slavers were paid on commission; every corpse was money lost. As a result, two schools of thought developed: the loose packers versus the tight packers.

The loose packers argued that by carrying slightly fewer slaves in slightly better conditions, more would survive and would reach port in better condition for market. The tight packers argued that a certain amount of wastage was unavoidable, so it was better to carry as much as possible; and even if rather more cargo died than in the loose packers' ships, there would still be more of it left alive, overall, at the other end. Some of the cargo would be in poor shape, but what of it? They could always be fattened up in the slave yard for a week or two before market. In general the tight packers won the argument. Slaving was a risky venture which brought big profits on each slave landed. It made sense to load all you could. And suppose you loose-packed them and none died? Think of all that space gone to waste ...

Slaving was a highly dangerous business, and only the lure of big money kept it going. When there was a war on, the slavers ran the gauntlet of French or Spanish warships; when there was no war, the West African coast was still plagued with pirates and privateers. The Slave Coast itself was completely lawless: ships from half-a-dozen nations competed for cargo in an atmosphere of suspicion and distrust, while the freelance agents ashore and the native slave-raiders manoeuvred to get the best prices. The basic drives were greed, hatred and fear, and occasionally fear triumphed. In 1759 an English sloop was up the River Gambia, searching for slaves, when natives attacked her and wounded the captain. Rather than be captured he fired his pistol into the powder magazine and blew up the whole ship.

The whole of the Middle Passage was dangerous. As one owner warned the captain: 'Let always a constant and careful watch be appointed ... for the preservation of their own lives as well as yours ... which per sleeping in their watches often proves fatal ...'. It proved fatal to Captain Holliday in May 1728: the slaves got loose and murdered all the crew except the cabin boy (perhaps they thought Holliday had been treating him as badly as them). In 1752 the *Marlborough* of Bristol was three days out from Africa with 400 negroes in chains when the captain brought 28 of them up on deck to help manage the ship. At the same time he sent some of the crew below to wash down the slaves. It was an unwise move. The negroes grabbed some firearms and before the day was over, 35 of the crew were dead. In the end the ex-slaves allowed

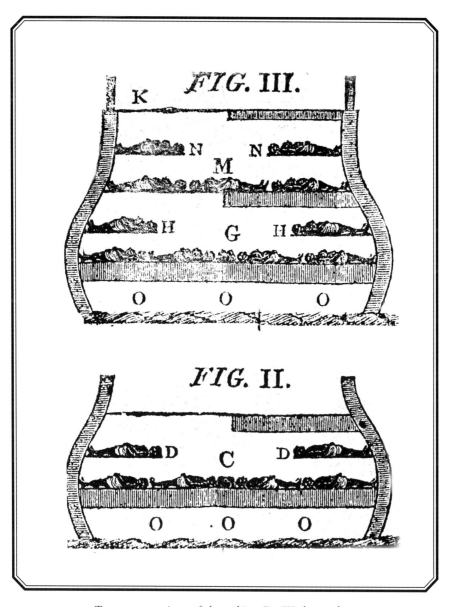

Two cross-sections of slave ships. Fig III shows slaves
carried in four layers; Fig II in two layers. Space between
the layers was 30 inches, sometimes only 20.
Ventilation was minimal.

the bosun and seven others to live – provided they navigated the
Marlborough back to Africa.

But it was exceptional for the negro to get a chance like that. If
he didn't die at sea he was sold to a plantation-owner; and many
of those were Bristolians, too. Black slaves seemed like God's gift
to Bristol and the horrific death toll was brushed aside as if it were
just another outbreak of fowl pest. In 1767 John Pinney sailed
in the *Bristol Merchant* for the island of Nevis, to take over the
family estates. 'I can assure you,' he wrote home, 'I was shocked
at the first appearance of human flesh for sale.' But the logical
consequences of that kind of thinking were too tough for him, and
he rapidly anaesthetized his conscience with this stunning piece
of claptrap: 'But surely God ordained them for use and benefit of
us; otherwise his Divine Will would have been manifest by some
particular sign or token.' Nothing short of a fiery message in the
sky reading *Hands Off Black Slaves, Bristol – Signed, God* would
have persuaded those Bristolian merchants to think again.

The remarkable thing is not that so few Bristolians had any
scruples about slaving but that so many of them were so hugely
confident that they were doing God's work. The ship owners threw
His name about as if the Almighty were on the board of directors.
They declared that the captain held office 'under God', that the
vessel sailed 'under God's grace', that the slaves were 'shipped
by the grace of God'. The Reverend John Newton – a friend of
Cowper's – studied for the ministry while captaining a slave ship.
The Society for the Promotion of Christian Knowledge (which
Colston joined in 1709) inherited two Barbados plantations in
1710 and not only kept 300 slaves working there but imported
fresh slaves every year to keep the numbers up.

How, then, did these educated, prosperous, Christian Englishmen
justify treating humans like animals, or worse than animals? How
could they live with the knowledge of so much needless suffering
and death? The quick and easy answer is that they did not consider
Africans to be human; Africans were sub-humans, objects, things
which bred like beasts and which belonged to anyone who found
them or who bought them. This lofty, casual outlook is nicely

caught in a letter of 1769 from Henry Laurens in South Carolina to Henry Bright & Co. of Bristol. He completes his report on his latest sale of slaves with a few words about the trifling losses, ending: 'a third poor pining creature hanged herself with a small piece of Vine which shews that her carcass was not very weighty.' Laurens mentions the incident only because the vine was small and the 'carcass' emaciated; the fact that a piece of his livestock had committed suicide was, in itself, commonplace.

It didn't take long for John Pinney's skin to grow just as thick. 'It is my son's wish to sell Jenetta's children,' he wrote to a friend, 'not herself, as she has done him so much injury, and begs you to let him know their value ...' There is a haunting blend of spite and practicality here which gives the lie to the 'quick and easy answer' suggested above. Bristolians could tell each other that African natives were not human, but those who spent a great part of their lives with slaves had to acknowledge their human nature, whether they liked it or not.

What's more, the evidence was here in Bristol too. Slaving captains were allowed to buy a couple of 'privileged slaves' for their own use, and they usually took one back to Bristol as a status symbol. You could tell a slaving captain by his flashy clothes – the coat dripping with lace, the hat too big and too cocked, the buttons and buckles ostentatiously expensive – and by his personal black slave, sometimes wearing a silver collar engraved with the owner's name. The Bristol newspapers often offered individual slaves for sale, or announced rewards for runaway slaves, some no older than ten. In July 1790 Hannah More heard the town crier going through the streets of Bristol, advertising the reward of a guinea for 'a poor negro girl who had run away because she would not return to one of those trafficking islands whither her master was resolved to send her ... the poor trembling wretch was dragged out from a hole in the top of a house where she had hid herself, and forced on board ship'. Nobody in Bristol pretended that these negroes were not human. In 1768 a Captain Read, of Frenchay, even announced in the *Bristol Journal* that he had *not* murdered his negro servant, whatever people might say.

The date of the beginning of the end of the slave trade is usually taken as June 1787. That was when the Reverend Thomas Clarkson rode into Bristol to start a fact-finding tour of the slaving ports. His investigation blew the lid off the whole business; yet in retrospect we can see that the lid came off with a bang because the rotting mess beneath it had built up so much pressure. In effect, what killed the slave trade was its own degrading, profiteering nature.

The ship owners preferred to use small vessels for slaving, because these could get in and out of shallow waters. On the other hand, small ships had small holds, so the owners ordered 'tight packing'. But tight packing encouraged disease, and on a long voyage the crew was bound to suffer with the cargo. Slavers became so notorious for sickness that it was hard to find a crew and impossible to keep one. To compensate for this, slaving captains turned their brutality and ruthlessness on to the crew – and it was *this* cruelty which first brought the trade under attack. The British public couldn't stand to think that British sailors were being ill treated, and when the facts were exposed, the suffering of the slaves came to light with them.

All of which is not to deny that Clarkson did a tremendous job. Before 1787 a few Bristol people (mainly Quakers) had opposed slaving, but more as a gesture than as a campaign. Clarkson got things organized. First he gathered all the information he could find. There was no shortage: everyone in Bristol knew something about the trade or the plantations. The clergy were either indifferent to him or hostile; the slaving companies and their captains refused to meet him or tried to sabotage his enquiries. But by hanging around the quays and listening to conversations in sailors' pubs, Clarkson eventually pieced together a fairly accurate picture.

For instance, he found that crews were recruited in three ways. First, by straightforward lying: the slaver's officers went to the drinking dens in Marsh Street and trapped any young sailor who was fool enough to swallow their stories of high wages and exotic sights. Second, by doping: they spiked a sailor's drink, bribed the landlord, and had the body dumped on board. Third, by blackmail: the landlord encouraged a sailor to get into debt and then threatened him with gaol – unless he joined the slaver. Once the crew was on board they had to sign the ship's articles without having read them, thus legalizing their poor wages – often paid in devalued colonial currency, just to complete the swindle.

The crew hated the captain and the captain despised the crew. Once at sea he had virtual power of life and death over them; often it was death. The slaver *Alfred* had just returned to Bristol when Clarkson arrived. The crew told him how the captain's cruelty had brought about the death of two seamen. Others told him about the slaver *Brothers,* lying off the mouth of the Avon. On a previous trip, *thirty-two* of her crew had died from ill treatment. During that voyage the captain had fastened a negro slave facedown on the deck, poured hot pitch on his back, and snipped the flesh with hot tongs.

There was no secret about these atrocities; they were openly discussed all over Bristol. Clarkson dug deeper and got hold of the crew lists for Bristol slavers. They showed that more seamen died 'in three slave vessels in a given time than in all (other) Bristol vessels put together, numerous as they were'. He found plenty of evidence to damn the slave trade, but no evidence that Bristol was ready to do without it. 'Everybody seemed to execrate it,' he said afterwards, 'but no one thought of its abolition.'

For a start, he tried to kick up a fuss over the deaths of the seamen. Burges, the deputy town clerk, urged him to forget it: even if the case ever got to court, he said, all the witnesses would disappear; the slaving merchants would see to that. Besides, Burges went on, it would be an endless task; he himself 'only knew of one captain from the port in the slave trade who did not deserve long ago to be hanged'. Clarkson rejected the advice and soldiered on alone.

At last, after a great deal of probing, he decided that he had enough good witnesses to prove that the mate of the slaver *Thomas* had ill-treated a seaman to death. When the case came up there were two slaving merchants on the bench. The slave-ship owners pooh-poohed the charge and said it was all 'hatched up by vagabonds';

but the evidence was too strong even for these biased magistrates, and they committed the mate for trial. As Burges had predicted, Clarkson's witnesses dropped out of sight when the assize opened. It didn't matter: the case had roused so much interest that the slave trade was beginning to be discussed all over the country.

The next year – 1788 – Parliament debated abolishing the trade. Bristol shuddered with indignation and warned that 'the ruin of thousands' would follow. 'Any check to the ample supply of this article,' declared the sugar-and-slave tycoons of Bristol in a petition to Parliament, 'would not only be ruinous in the extreme to the petitioners engaged in the manufacture but the mischief would extend most widely, throwing many hundreds of common labouring people ... wholly out of employment.' Without the slave trade 'the cultivation of the West India colonies cannot be carried on', and 'the decline of the trade of the City of Bristol must inevitably follow'; indeed, the merchants implied that they themselves might be left starving in the gutter: 'instead of contributing largely as at present to the burdens of the State, (they) must look up to the public for relief'. It was all very moving. In the end Parliament merely passed an Act to reduce the suffering of slaves carried by British ships, mainly by controlling their numbers. Mr Brickdale, M.P. for Bristol, voted against it.

The debate had revealed many things not mentioned by the petitioners. A former surgeon on a slaver told the House of Commons that his ship had carried loads of over 600 slaves. A slaver captain gave evidence that he allocated 5½ feet by 16 inches per slave. Another captain testified that on one voyage he lost 15 out of 40 seamen and 120 out of 360 slaves. Wilberforce, the leading abolitionist in Parliament, came back to the attack in 1789, and again Bristol countered with a flurry of petitions. 'The abolition of the slave trade ... will deprive the Port of Bristol of so great a share of its present commerce ... that it will involve thousands in the utmost difficulty and distress.' So boomed the voice of big business in Bristol. When the first abolitionist committee to be formed outside London met in Bristol, the Establishment retaliated by forming its own committee to defend the slave trade 'on which the

VALUABLE

ARTICLES

FOR THE

Slave Trade

To be SOLD at and under Prime Coft, in Confe-
quence of the EXPECTED ABOLITION.

ABOUT Ten Million Dozen Negro Guns, at 24s. per Doz
About Three Tons Weight Hand and Feet Shackles and Thumb
Screws, at $1\frac{1}{2}$d. per Pound; About Ten Thoufand Fine Gold-
Laced Hats, at $10\frac{1}{2}$d. each; Ten Thoufand Grofs Negro Knives,
he whole caft Iron, at 14s. per Grofs; About Three Tons bril-
liant Diamond Necklaces, at 3s. per Pound; About Ten Thou-
fand Pieces fine Negro Linen, at $5\frac{1}{2}$d. Drawback $1\frac{1}{2}$d. per Yd.
About Ten Thoufand Doz. Negro Looking Glaffes, at 3s. per
Doz. And Five Thoufand Quarters Horfe-Beans, at a very reduced Price.

Enquire of the Slave Mongers.

☞ SPCIMENS of the Whole (except the Thumb Screws, the
Sight of which it is thought would too-deeply wound the Feel-
ings of thofe not inclined to purchafe) are NOW exhibiting
on the Exchange.

*Bristol slavers in a dilemma. Who wants 'valuable' shackles
when the slave trade is ending? Note that nervous customers
need not see the thumbscrews. A sensitive city, Bristol.*

welfare of the West India islands and the commerce and revenue of the kingdom so essentially depend'. Note which came first; there was a lot of Bristol money in the West Indies. Most of the men on this committee were members of the Corporation, including an alderman who once captained a slaver. When the House of Commons rejected one of Wilberforce's motions, they had the church bells rung in Bristol.

Bristol was making all this noise because it was on the defensive. Wilberforce had begun to get public opinion behind him, and the slave-merchants' cause wasn't helped by a piece of crude bullying on the Slave Coast in 1791. Three Bristol ships – the *Wasp*, the *Thomas* and the *Recovery* – with three other English slavers tried to force down the price of slaves by threatening to bombard the town of Calabar. When there was no reply the six vessels opened fire and pounded Calabar for several hours. In the Commons, Wilberforce used the event to pound his opponents: the sole purpose of the slaughter, he said, was to help a few Bristol and Liverpool merchants make a few hundred pounds more profit.

The merchants ignored him, but the people listened. Even Bristolians began to have an uneasy feeling that perhaps the slave trade had distorted their sense of values and soiled their city's honour. In 1806, when Parliament voted to abolish the slave trade, Bristol's howl of anguish was fairly small. But then, so was its share of the business. Any suggestion that Bristol's slavers gave in graciously is far off the mark. The reason why they didn't fight more strenuously to defend the slave trade was that by then, most of it had gone to Liverpool.

Bristol steadily pulled out of slave-trading after about 1750. Between 1756 and 1786, Bristol sent 588 ships to the Slave Coast; Liverpool sent 1,858. By the time Wilberforce's campaign was gathering momentum, Bristol had no more than half-a-dozen ships out slaving. Between 1795 and 1804 they made a mere 29 voyages, while Liverpool's slavers were totalling 1,009 voyages.

This shift away from slaving had nothing to do with conscience or scruples. It was pure business. Slaving was lucrative but risky, and it meant sailing a long, three-cornered route. The direct there-and-back route to the West Indies was faster, safer and by this time almost as profitable. Besides, many Bristol families owned sugar plantations and they preferred to trade with their own people. Long before 1807, most Bristol slave merchants had got their money out of ships and into West Indian estates. When slavery itself was abolished in 1833 many Bristolians received quite huge amounts in compensation from the Government. One Bristol firm – Messrs Thomas & John Daniel – got £55,178 for their own slaves, plus a great deal more for slaves on estates mortgaged to them; all told, they collected nearly a quarter of a million pounds. Bristol did very nicely out of every aspect of slavery – even its abolition.

In recent years it has become fashionable among historians to play down the atrocity of the slave trade by putting forward one (or both) of two excuses. The first excuse is that the slave-traders lived in an age with completely different moral standards, and that by *their* lights they were decent, honourable men doing a necessary job. The second excuse is that, okay, maybe they went a bit too far, but who are we to talk when our own generation has produced more than its share of mass horror? Neither excuse stands up.

Moral standards do change – but they don't turn upside-down within 80 or 90 years. If the slave trade was full of sincere, well-meaning citizens in, say, 1705, what had happened to make them change their views by 1795? The trade itself hadn't changed: it was just as filthy and barbarous at the start as it was at the finish. The death rate hadn't changed: the Middle Passage consistently killed off tens of thousands of slaves a year. Public knowledge of the vileness of the trade certainly increased as the century wore on, but are we seriously expected to believe that people in Bristol were never fully aware, from the start, of the squalid side of the business which brought back so much wealth? The port was full of slavers and the pubs were full of seamen; only the deaf, the blind or the blinkered could avoid learning at least some of the facts.

The truth is that Bristolians made too much money out of the slave trade to *want* to change it – and once profit has become your god it's a fairly simple step to assume that God has planned that profit. What's more, because the suffering was happening a long way off, they somehow felt less responsible for it. To say that their moral standards were different is an easy way out. When they were forced to face up to the sickening reality of the trade, their moral standards turned out to be very like ours. If the slaving community in Bristol deserves any epitaph, it is this: *They did it for the money.*

The second excuse is quickly knocked down. Inhumanity in our century does not diminish or disguise inhumanity in any other century. We don't try to gloss over the atrocities of Dachau, the massacres in Rwanda or the devastation of Vietnam. There is no reason why we should hesitate to condemn the slave trade. It happened, and it was evil.

To end with, here is a reminder of how evil it could be – and of the way in which violence tends to brutalize those who use it. One of the Pinney family took a partner for his West Indian plantations. They drew up an agreement which stipulated that when a slave died he was to be replaced by the partner who owned him, *'except such slaves as shall be killed by the cruelty of the other party'*. Signed, sealed and settled with a handshake. They probably had a glass of Bristol Milk to celebrate.

CHAPTER FIVE

---◆---

IT WAS
A RIOT

---◆---

The Bristol Riots of 1831 had everything. Starting with the threat of tyranny and the spur of hunger, they worked through violent demonstrations, attempted murder, tumult, riot, gaol-breaking, arson, looting, mass drunkenness, total anarchy, sabre-charges, street-fighting, deaths by the dozen and damage running into millions. Add for good measure the suicidal apathy of the Corporation and the mysterious paralysis of the local troops, and you have a mixture as rich as any banana-republic revolt.

So it's worth looking at the background to it all.

On the face of it, the Bristol Riots were about the reform of Parliament: whether or not all M.P.s should be elected by their constituents (or at least by some of them) instead of, in many cases, being appointed by wealthy patrons who controlled 'rotten boroughs' – constituencies with few voters, sometimes none at all. Well, reform was important, and the rioters shouted for it loud and long, but oddly enough Bristol was one of the places least in need of it. In 1831 the city already had two M.P.s, both pro-reform, and when the Reform Bill was passed in 1832 it made little difference to the number of voters in the city. By the standards of the day, Bristol's voting lists were pretty big. Reform certainly made no difference to the rioters. They were poor. Only the well-to-do voted.

So there had to be other reasons for the explosion. One was hard times. The West Indian trade was running down, now that it was clear that slavery would soon be abolished, and the port of Bristol was steadily pricing itself out of the market. As usual, the unskilled suffered most. When a labourer got work he made between 1s 6d (7½p) and half-a-crown (12½p) a day; but a quartern loaf cost anything from ninepence to a shilling (4p to 5p) or more, and such things as tea at five shillings (25p) a pound were far beyond him. And very many labourers were out of work.

Moreover, there was a jumpy nervousness everywhere. In 1830 the French had brought off a bloodless revolution, and many Englishmen envied their success. In 1831 cholera got into the northern coal-ports and started spreading south; it encouraged a doomsday mentality, a hysterical feeling that the end of the world was at hand and so 'anything goes'. When the House of Lords threw out the Reform Bill on 8th October, Bristol wasn't the first place to erupt: in Derby the mob stormed the prison and in Nottingham they burned the castle. But when trouble *did* hit Bristol the damage was far worse, because the city despised the Corporation, the Corporation distrusted the mayor, and nobody in authority wanted to be the one who ended up with blood on his hands.

To appreciate the contempt which the average ratepayer felt for the Corporation you have to understand how that body was elected, and who it represented. The mayor was elected by the council. The aldermen were elected by the mayor and the other aldermen. The councillors were elected (for life) by the council, who also elected the sheriffs and the chamberlain. In other words, the members of the Corporation represented nobody but themselves. They certainly didn't consider themselves the servants of the public; quite the opposite. 'They add insolence to oppression', reported one citizen, 'and carry themselves with such haughtiness towards the inhabitants as renders them odious and disgusting.' When the riots began, and the aldermen – who were also the magistrates – appealed for help in protecting Corporation property, it's little wonder that they got a frosty answer.

And then there was Sir Charles Wetherell, M.P.

The man was a bit of a buffoon. He belonged to the rant-and-rave school of political speaking, and because he never wore a belt or braces, the House of Commons was usually so fascinated by the widening gap between his waistcoat and his breeches that it didn't pay much attention to his remarks; not that they needed much attention, because Wetherell was the kind of politician who is always violently *against* things.

In 1829 he had been violently against the Bill to give civil rights to Roman Catholics. This made him, for a while, wildly popular in Bristol. He was Attorney General and Recorder of the city, and when he came down to hold the assize the mob shouted 'Wetherell for ever!' (they also smashed the reformist mayor's windows and destroyed a Catholic chapel in Trenchard Street). This seems to have given Wetherell the impression that Bristol agreed with him on all subjects, including the reform of Parliament. Throughout 1831 he boomed away in the Commons, making in all 180 speeches against Reform, and too often he claimed to be speaking for Bristol. In April 1831, when he came to hold the assize, Bristol had put him straight, and done it loud and clear. Wetherell ignored the message. He went back to Westminster and told the House that 'the Reform fever had a good deal abated in Bristol': this from a man who didn't even *represent* Bristol – he had been given one of four 'rotten' seats in Yorkshire which the Duke of Newcastle owned.

Everybody knew that, next time, Wetherell would get a much hotter reception, one that he couldn't ignore. The situation worsened after the Lords rejected the Bill. The anti-Reformers were stupid enough to do a bit of gloating in public, so the Reformers held a huge and noisy meeting in Queen Square. Wetherell answered with a typically frenzied speech in the House of Commons. On 24th October the Bishop of Bath and Wells (who had voted against the Bill) came to Bristol to consecrate the new church of St Paul, in Coronation Road. He had to be protected against the anger of the locals, and afterwards he drove off at full gallop, with volleys of stones bouncing off his carriage.

By now the Corporation was worried about Wetherell, who was due in Bristol in a week's time. They asked the Government for troops to protect him (and them). Only 93 soldiers were provided: two troops of the 14th Dragoons, quartered at Clifton, and one troop of the 3rd Dragoon Guards at Keynsham. The aldermen had made an effort to recruit seamen from the port as an extra bodyguard, but the sailors said they 'would not allow themselves to be made catspaws by the Corporation'. Next, the aldermen tried to swear in 300 special constables, but got such little response – only 200 applicants turned up, mostly young hotheads and rabid Tories – that they were forced to enrol a hundred toughs with experience as stewards at elections; they were known as 'bludgeon men'. The Corporation had tried to postpone the assize; Wetherell wouldn't hear of it. Now there was nothing to do but hope for the best.

Wetherell usually opened the assize in the afternoon, but on Saturday 29th October 1831 his private carriage trundled along the Bath Road at half-past ten in the morning. It made no difference: the crowds were waiting for him, over a thousand strong. He stopped at Totterdown to transfer to the civic coach, and 'was instantly assailed by the most deafening yells, groans and hisses'. The coach moved off, surrounded by constables and followed by the mob. The journey to the Guildhall was rowdy and at times dangerous; as the coach crossed Bristol Bridge a stone laid open a special constable's head – the first of countless casualties to come. Wetherell went into the Guildhall through 'a whirlwind of yells'.

The courtroom was in uproar from the start. The Clerk of the Arraigns couldn't make himself heard. The Recorder threatened to commit anyone making a disturbance. The tumult increased. After tremendous noise and confusion, Sir Charles adjourned the court until Monday morning. Or so he thought.

Now Wetherell had to be driven in the mayor's coach to the Mansion House in Queen Square. As before, the hooting and howling were continuous. There was an attempt to capsize the coach at the foot of Clare Street, and it was briefly stoned when it reached the Mansion House, but both men got indoors without being hurt. The other magistrates hurried after them. They all thought the worst was over. The crowd outside numbered two or three thousand, but many soon drifted away, and the magistrates actually relaxed enough to discuss whether or not they should have a civic procession to church the next day. Meanwhile they left the protesters to the special constables. The specials had been spoiling for a fight all along, but the mayor had ordered them to concentrate on protecting the Recorder, and many had the bruises to prove it. As soon as Wetherell was safe, they began getting their own back.

It was a great mistake. The people they pounded with their staves were not necessarily the troublemakers, and the ones they arrested were simply the ones they could catch; what's more their obvious pleasure in knocking people about soon infuriated the crowd. The specials made enemies out of spectators and revived the disturbance just as it was dying. For two or three hours there were running fights all over the Square, and one of the constables was actually chased into the Float. At about three o'clock a group of prisoners was sent to Bridewell under escort. Some of the mob cut them off in Nelson Street, knocked down the constables and set the prisoners free. One constable was kicked repeatedly in the head.

By now the specials had been on duty for seven or eight hours. A large number of them went home for food and rest. The crowd simply saw the specials retreating, and celebrated this by charging through the few who remained. They ripped down the railings in front of the Mansion House and flung bricks through the ground-floor windows. The fight was on again.

At last the mayor showed himself. Charles Pinney was not personally unpopular – he was in favour of Reform – but he was no great leader either. He warned, he pleaded, and he got a shower of stones in return. (A rock just missed his head.) By now it was dusk. He stood on a chair and read the Riot Act, three times. This meant that a state of riot now officially existed; the law directed that if twelve or more persons refused to disperse and remained together for an hour, they were liable to the death penalty. The mob howled derision and renewed its attack with a furious bombardment of brickbats and broken masonry. 'Give us the bloody Recorder,' they roared, 'we'll murder him!'

The constables had either been driven indoors, or disarmed and beaten up (one was forced to throw his staff through the windows), so the Mansion House was now vulnerable. The rioters got some heavy beams, battered in the doors and windows, and swarmed through the ground floor, smashing furniture, mirrors and chandeliers as they went. They drove the cooks from the kitchen and grabbed the civic feast: joints, fowls, game and pies were 'liberated', to huge cheers from the spectators. The mayor's party had barricaded themselves in the upper rooms and were putting up a stiff fight. The rioters piled straw and faggots in the dining room and got ready to burn down the house, and the Recorder with it.

At last the troops appeared.

We can only guess at the magistrates' reluctance to call them in much earlier. Maybe they were afraid that force would only provoke more force; maybe they doubted whether 93 soldiers were enough; probably they all wanted somebody else to make a decision which might turn out to be *(a)* foolish, *(b)* unnecessary or *(c)* the cause of bloodshed. Whatever the reason, their sluggishness nearly got them all burned to a crisp. The only thing that held the attackers back was their failure to find a light (matches hadn't been invented yet) and they were still looking for one when Lieutenant-Colonel Brereton led two troops of horse soldiers into Queen Square.

Five minutes earlier, Wetherell had escaped. He scrambled across the flat roof of the dining room, climbed a ladder into the window of the next house, and made his way to the stables on Little King Street, at the rear. He swapped clothes with a coachman and walked away through the crowd. By morning he was in Newport. The cause of the trouble had gone – but it was much harder to make a riot stop than to let it start; especially with a man like Brereton in command of the troops.

The arrival of the soldiers was enough to get the rioters out of the Mansion House. Brereton met the magistrates and the mayor, who told him to clear the Square, using whatever force he thought necessary. Brereton was against the use of any force at all. He said he thought they were a 'good-humoured mob' and would go away if he simply 'walked his troops about', and that was what he ordered them to do.

One of Brereton's problems was that he knew a lot of the rioters by sight, and they knew him. He'd been living at Redfield House in St George's for the past three years; many of his neighbours were in Queen Square that Saturday night. Everywhere he went the mob cheered him and people shook his hand. It must be difficult for an officer to cope with that sort of riot, especially when the officer is 49, semi-retired, and hasn't seen action for the best part of 20 years. Brereton tried to jolly the mob. The mob jollied him back,

Poor Brereton. Neither he nor his horse looks comfortable.
When he couldn't disperse the mob, he went to bed.

but they pelted his men with stones and bits of iron. Two dragoons were badly hurt and an officer was injured when his horse fell.

By 11 p.m. it was obvious that Brereton's 'low-profile' policy wasn't going to work. The Square was still full of rioters and the rioters were still full of old buck. At last Brereton told Captain Gage's troop of the 14th Dragoons to charge – but he ordered the men to strike only with the flat of their sabres. The charge scattered the mob, but they hid in alleys or on barges where the soldiers couldn't follow, and kept up their stone throwing. Gage led his troop back to the Mansion House and asked for orders to fire. Brereton wouldn't give the order without direct instructions from the mayor, and the mayor wasn't willing to take that responsibility alone. For a while it was stalemate: the dragoons and the constables held the Mansion House and the middle of the Square; the mob held the alleys and backstreets. There was a grim moment when a gang of men boarded a trow in the harbour and demanded a carboy of vitriol to throw over the soldiers' horses, but just at that moment the dragoons rode by. The rioters ran off to stone them, and the captain of the trow took his chance to move his boat to the middle of the Float.

At about a quarter to midnight, part of the mob abandoned the sport in the Square and went off to break the windows of the Council House, which stood by the Guildhall on Corn Street and Broad Street. They had smashed about a hundred panes when Captain Gage's troop rode up. Gage's orders were to do what he thought necessary to protect the Council House, so he promptly charged the rioters and chased them through High Street, Broad Street and Wine Street. This time the edge of the sabre was used, and used vigorously. Eight people were badly hurt. The rioters pelted the troops from alleys which the horses couldn't enter, and there was some firing. One report says that Gage tried to shoot a ringleader in Wine Street but his pistol misfired and a trooper shot the man instead; another report described the victim as 'a peaceful ostler returning from his stable'. Whichever version you prefer, the result was the same: one corpse, much blood, and no rioters to be seen. Gage had completely cleared the streets.

For a few hours the city was fairly quiet. At 2 a.m. the troops went to their quarters, leaving pickets on guard at the Mansion House and the Council House. Carpenters worked through the night, boarding up the windows and doors of the Mansion House. The mayor and one of the sheriffs stayed on duty. All the other members of the Corporation went home. So did most of the special constables. They had been organized on Saturday evening by Major Digby Mackworth (who happened to be in Bristol after leading a punitive expedition to the Forest of Dean, where the farm labourers were giving trouble). He came back to the Square at dawn on Sunday to find his force of 250 specials 'had dwindled to a dozen, and were even then diminishing in number'. Brereton arrived and decided that the pickets must have rest. He ordered them to their quarters. The Square was again defenceless. Before long the rioters discovered this.

By 8 a.m. the mob was in action, ripping the boards off the doors of the Mansion House and stealing or smashing everything they found inside, including Wetherell's judicial robe and wig, which were torn to bits and handed out as souvenirs. The mayor, Major Mackworth and some constables retreated upstairs. They got out by an attic window and ran, crouching, between the double roofs of eight or nine houses until they reached the Custom House, where they kicked in a window and made their way down to the street. The mayor went in search of Colonel Brereton and told him the bad news. The cavalry saddled up again and back they went to Queen Square, where one major change had taken place. The rioters had found the Mansion House cellars, and they were drunk.

It was the start of the biggest free orgy in the history of Bristol. Already several hundred bottles of the Corporation's port, sherry and madeira were being emptied down throats hoarse from much rioting. Those who could stand were staggering, cursing, singing. Those who had fallen down were rolling about. Those who had got there first were paralytic. The good word was spreading rapidly through the city: free booze in Queen Square! The mob grew, and as it grew its character changed. All the layabouts and tearaways

Queen Square in the hands of the mob - and Bristol at the mercy of the flames.

in town turned up, looking for a chance to chuck a brick and pinch a bottle – in the name of Reform.

The constables and cavalry recaptured the Mansion House. An alderman read the Riot Act yet again, but Brereton still refused to let his men fire; they were exhausted and outnumbered, he said, and shooting would only infuriate the mob, who were already very hostile to the 14th Dragoons for killing that rioter in Wine Street last night. Indeed at about 10.30 a.m. Brereton ordered the 14th back to their quarters near College Green, and the mob, naturally, regarded that as a victory. About 500 of them followed and stoned the soldiers. The troop halted and drew swords; six dragoons charged the length of Prince Street. This action cleared the way and the troop went on along the Quay.

In those days the Harbour stretched right up through what is now the Centre, nearly as far as Christmas Steps, with a drawbridge across it more or less where Burke's statue now stands. The mob ran down Marsh Street and got to the drawbridge first; the troops took another pelting there, and were harassed all along the quay on the other side. Opposite Denmark Street a dozen rioters tried to drag a soldier from his horse; he shot one man dead. The mob fell back, but they went on stoning, accurately and painfully. The dragoons fired shots on their way up to College Green and hit seven or eight people. Some rioters had run through Denmark Street and up Unity Street, but the dragoons cleared them out. Others tried stoning from the middle of the Green until they were chased away.

The news that the 14th had fired again made Brereton very unhappy. Despite the magistrates' opposition he insisted that the 14th must immediately get out of the city, and he went to their stables to give the order personally. According to Captain Gage, Brereton's words were: 'Captain Gage, march your squadron immediately out of Bristol; if you do not, the whole squadron will be murdered.' There was a short delay while Gage assembled his men. Brereton became agitated: 'For God's sake, Captain Gage, will you get out of town?' Gage asked where they were to go. 'Anywhere you please, only go away,' Brereton said. Keynsham was suggested. Brereton agreed, as long as they hurried: 'You must trot out of town,' he ordered. The Squadron rode out by Hotwell Road, Cumberland Basin and the Bath Road – a six-mile trip for men and horses who Brereton had said were too tired to tackle the rioters.

As soon as they had gone, Brereton went to Queen Square. The mob cheered him and he made a short speech. The 14th had been sent away, he announced, and there would be no more firing. He begged everyone to go home. It was not a promising formula, and it didn't work. The 3rd Dragoons were guarding the wine cellars but there was enough drink in the Square to keep everyone happy. The mob still believed the Recorder was in the Mansion House, and they still wanted his head.

Meanwhile, life went on. Queen Square – cut off by water on three sides – was an isolated spot, of course, but it seems as if most of Bristol simply didn't want to know about the Corporation's problems. While rioters were swigging the mayor's drink outside the wreckage of the Mansion House, the rest of Bristol went to church and chapel as usual. Nearly all the congregations, perhaps 20,000 people in all, heard a mayoral appeal for help read out; only about 200 men answered it. The turnout was so poor that the volunteers decided to go home, try to recruit friends and neighbours, and meet again at three.

This was not public apathy; it was public contempt. If the Corporation behaved like a private monopoly and ignored public opinion, it couldn't expect the public to care when it got into trouble.

By midday the mayor had issued placards announcing that Sir Charles Wetherell had left the city. Nobody believed it. The placards were torn down and the bill-sticker was knocked about; he ended up with his paste-pot on his head. The mob in the Square went on watching and drinking. The soldiers of the 3rd Dragoons outside the Mansion House frightened nobody; hadn't Brereton hustled the 14th away because they fired? There was nothing to worry about. A rioter climbed the mounted statue of William III in the middle of the Square and hoisted a tricolour cap. 'The cap of liberty!' he cried. Thanks to the Corporation's excellent taste in wine, the crowd was enjoying itself.

It couldn't last. Ironically the man who ended the party was a Quaker. Mr Waring's intentions were of the best: he came to the Square at one o'clock and persuaded the leaders of the mob that Wetherell really had left. Waring hoped that the crowd would go home. Instead, they went to Bridewell to release the prisoners arrested the previous night.

This was where the day began to go utterly to hell.

Bridewell prison stood where Bridewell police station now stands, but in those days it straddled Bridewell Lane. The gaol was on one side, and the gaoler's house on the other. Two strong archways linked them; a heavy gate closed each arch. The gaoler, Evans, and his two officers armed themselves with swords, but they couldn't stop the crowd heaving the gates off their hinges and tossing them into the Frome. Evans retreated indoors and thrust a blunderbuss out of a window. He kept the rioters at bay for fifteen minutes, but they had stolen some hammers and crowbars from a smith's shop in Nelson Street, and with these they forced an entry. Evans threw down the keys. His wife and children were in the house. He got them away over the rooftops, minutes before the rioters (having freed the prisoners) set fire to the gaol and the chapel.

During this attack, Evans had sent a message to the Guildhall, telling the aldermen that twenty constables and ten soldiers could still hold Bridewell. According to the messenger, the aldermen's comment was: 'You say they have released the prisoners. Pooh-pooh! There will be nothing more done.' Once again the Corporation was treating the facts, not as they were, but as they would like them to be.

All that day the Corporation behaved like men in never-never land. In the morning they snubbed an offer of help from 250 army pensioners, all disciplined veterans. At midday the mayor's appeal brought 200 volunteers to the Guildhall; nobody knew what to do with them. The volunteers came back at three o'clock and couldn't get in; nobody had told them that only a side door would be open. When at last the meeting started – by now Bridewell was in flames – the mayor was asked if he had a plan; no, he said, he hadn't. At this point the town clerk announced that he would speak for the magistrates. He gave the meeting the benefit of his lengthy political views, advised each man to 'act on his own discretion and responsibility', and sat down. Brereton was no help. He refused to recall the 14th, and he insisted that the 3rd were too tired to be used. Eventually the mayor decided that since it would soon be dark, the best they could do was each go home and take care of his own property. And this they did.

By then, the New Gaol was in flames.

The Corporation was very proud of this gaol, a massive, almost baronial building which had cost £60,000 – about £5,000,000 in today's money – and was only eleven years old. It stood on the land between the Float and the Cut, opposite Canons Marsh, with its main gates facing south (their ruins can still be seen alongside Cumberland Road).

The mob that marched on the gaol was well armed: 'most of them had bludgeons; some had hatchets; and others were armed with iron palisades'. More to the point, they had sledgehammers, crowbars and iron wedges. While they set to work on the big gates, the prison governor went to the Guildhall to seek instructions: should he defend the gaol, or release the prisoners? He was told to use his own discretion. The governor, two aldermen and about 60 citizens tried to reach the gaol, but the rioters drove them off with volleys of stones. By now there was a huge crowd on both sides of the Avon.

It took about 45 minutes to smash a hole in the gates. The rest was easy. A man crawled through and drew the bolts; within minutes about 300 rioters had the run of the gaol and 170 prisoners were free. (Many – men and women – celebrated their release by stripping off their prison clothes and running about naked.) But only three prisoners had actually got outside the walls when 20 of the 3rd Dragoons, led by Cornet Kelson, reached the prison gates. Kelson could see the mob 'knocking things to pieces' inside, and he could easily have shut the gates and trapped the lot of them. Instead he wheeled his men about and took them back to their quarters. For those had been Brereton's explicit orders: go to the gaol, and return. The rioters cheered the troops and shouted, 'The soldiers are with us!' The dragoons – no doubt wondering whose side they really were on – waved back.

Now the New Gaol was doomed. The mob sacked the governor's house and threw everything moveable – books, records, furniture – into the river. The tide was ebbing fast, so it all got swept away. They smashed what they couldn't move, and then set fire to the whole place. The governor's house, with the chapel above it, burned briskly; so did the treadmill and the gallows. It was a murky, drizzling afternoon: psychologically perfect conditions for burning a prison. The watching thousands were suitably awed, and the rioters immediately set off to give them something more to gape at. There were tollgates and tollhouses on the road at Cumberland Basin and at Prince Street Bridge. They threw the gates into the water and set the houses on fire. Then they headed for the third prison, the Gloucestershire House of Correction at Lawford's Gate, just beyond Old Market. That was child's play: they simply rang the bell and grabbed the turnkey when he opened the door. Within ten minutes the prisoners were unlocked from their irons and the gaol was blazing.

It was half past six, and all three prisons were on fire. At that moment the mob controlled Bristol. They went where they liked and did as they pleased, beating on doors, demanding drink or money, threatening arson or murder. The mayor couldn't, and Brereton wouldn't, do a thing. As one observer wrote, 'the city seemed given up to the lawless insolence and outrage of the most daring villains.' By half past seven the villains were at College Green, daring their biggest outrage yet: the firing of the Bishop's Palace.

Bishop Gray's vote had helped defeat the Reform Bill on 8th October. On this Sunday morning he had preached at the cathedral, despite warnings from friends that he should get out of town. 'It shall never be said of me,' he declared, 'that I turned my back on religion.' In the afternoon things worsened, and he left.

It was no secret that his palace was on the rioters' list; the mayor and magistrates got word that the mob was heading that way in time to organize a body of citizens and specials to defend it, and they sent a messenger to the stables with orders for the dragoons to meet them there. As usual, nothing worked out as planned. A gang of rioters – some say 100, some say 30 – arrived first, hoisted the palace-yard gates off their hinges and bashed the front door down. They raced through the building, smashing furniture, ripping open beds and scattering red-hot coals from the fires. Then the dragoons reached the Green, under Colonel Brereton's personal command, and the rioters took fright and ran.

Brereton's troops rode into the palace yard and formed up by the door. The mayor's men went through the palace, putting out the fires and chasing the rioters. There was some desperate fighting in the house and the gardens, and many looters escaped with plunder. The bishop's butler asked for the soldiers' help, and so did the constables. Brereton refused, and a few minutes later the men inside heard a tremendous cheer. The cavalry had gone.

By now the Green was packed with people, and the mob rushed the palace. They overwhelmed the defenders and sacked the place from cellar to attic, especially the cellar: episcopal claret was on sale at a penny or twopence a bottle that night. They fired the palace again, and this time it went up like a giant bonfire.

Most of the chapterhouse library – 6,000 books and valuable manuscripts – was thrown into the blaze. The palace burned so fast and so fiercely that the lead 'ran off the roof like water'. The rioters tried to set fire to the chapterhouse, but its Saxon stonework would not burn. They turned to the cathedral. The sub-sacrist, a Mr Phillips, barred their way, and three or four Nonconformist citizens had the courage to back him up; no Reformer, they said, would destroy the people's property; and the rioters went off to Reeves' Hotel, which was the dragoons' headquarters, and smashed its windows instead.

This was the point in the riots where farce began to enter the tragedy. Seven soldiers were in Queen Square, keeping the mob out of the Mansion House, when the warning came of an attack on the bishop's palace. They reached College Green to find the palace intact. Across the harbour, however, they saw the Mansion House spouting flames. Back they went to Queen Square. When they got there they were too late to save the Mansion House and just in time to see that the palace was ablaze.

The dragoons hung around for an hour or two, waiting for orders, which never came. The specials had all disappeared, the mob wouldn't let the firemen near the burning buildings, Brereton seemed to have lost his nerve or his wits, or both, and the magistrates were conspicuously elsewhere. The dragoons quit.

And that wasn't all. At ten o'clock the Dodington troop of

Gloucestershire Yeomanry arrived. The magistrates had sent for them and here they were, 40 strong and eager for orders. Captain Codrington, their commander, couldn't find a magistrate at the Council House. Eventually he found Colonel Brereton, watching the palace burn. Brereton said that without the presence of a magistrate he could give him no instructions. In Codrington's report to the Home Secretary he wrote that he 'paraded through the principal streets of the city for more than two hours, without being able to find a magistrate'. He saw no hope 'of being in any way serviceable, the city being actually in the uncontrolled power of the populace', so he took his troop back to Dodington. They reached home at five in the morning, having ridden the best part of 40 miles for nothing.

Shortly after talking to Codrington, Colonel Brereton went to bed, thus missing the colossal climax of the whole disastrous weekend.

Before the rioters fired the Mansion House they had emptied its cellars of about 7,000 bottles, and some spectacular drinking was going on in Queen Square. (Hospital records show that at least two people drank themselves to death.) After the flames took hold, a few of the looters were too drunk or too greedy to realize how fast the fire was spreading, and they got burned alive. Nevertheless, a lot of ambitious looting took place: six men carried out a new grand piano and sold it on the spot for four shillings.

The mob may have been drunk, but they knew good plunder when they saw it, and they also knew that with the soldiers in their quarters, nothing was impossible. They beat in the doors of the private houses next to the Mansion House, ransacked everything that was portable, smashed up the heavy furniture and set it on fire. Before midnight the range of eight or nine houses between the Mansion House and the Custom House was one long inferno. At midnight the Custom House officers got notice to quit. The mob swept upstairs and met a band of rioters who had escaped from the adjoining house by climbing on to the roof. Some of them found supper laid in the housekeeper's room, and they got stuck into it. Before they knew what was happening, the staircase was a

The riots at night, as seen from south of the river. Looters hurry over the bridge to get their share. Note that in 1831 St Mary Redcliffe had no spire.

mass of flames and they were trapped. All died. Others were killed when they jumped from the windows. At least one man fell on to the roof of the portico and was roasted alive in the molten lead.

None of this discouraged the survivors. They worked their way along the rest of the north side and by 1 a.m. the entire row was burning. The flames spread to some warehouses in King Street, including a bonded store whose rum barrels burst and poured a wall of fire down the street. Then the rioters moved across the road to the *west* side, and burned that too. By now most of the adults were too drunk to commit arson, and a gang of 50 boys dashed from house to house with burning brands. An eye-witness described how three boys, each ten or eleven years old, were trapped in an attic 'and while the flames were bursting out beneath them, coolly clambered along a coping projecting not more than three inches, and, entering an adjoining house, immediately set fire to a bedstead and furniture'. A rioter who sat in a drawing-room window, cheering the mob, had worse luck. The house was on fire, and when the smoke reached his window he fell on to the spikes of the court wall, where for a long time he lay impaled until the joke wore off and the crowd prised him free.

The west side of the Square created an even more terrific blaze than the north side, because it contained the Customs Bonding-warehouse and many cellars full of spirit; it was like one long liquid-fuel dump. By three in the morning, half of Queen Square was burning, together with much of Prince Street, King Street, the bishop's palace and what was left of the three gaols – a scene of fiery devastation not to be matched until the nights of the blitz. Charles Kingsley, then at boarding school on St Michael's Hill, watched 'the red reflected glare till it arched itself into one vast dome of red-hot iron ... and beneath it, miles away, I could see the lovely tower of Dundry, shining red'. So much of Bristol was on fire that a man at Beachley, near Chepstow, claimed the glow in the sky was bright enough to let him read a book in his garden. It was sheer luck that the fire didn't spread across King Street to Marsh Street and into the ancient part of the city. If there hadn't been a steady drizzle, or if there had been a fresh breeze, the flames would have swept irresistibly through those crowded old buildings. Bristol was saved by a meteorological accident.

The scene in Queen Square was like a Hollywood reconstruction for an epic to be called *Sodom and Gomorrah Go To Hell And Back,* with a cast not of thousands but of tens of thousands. The orgy had grown into a debauch. Whenever the drink ran low, the rioters simply beat in somebody's door and rolled out a fresh barrel of wine or beer. The looting was prodigious, and the Square looked like an enormous open-air auction. A shilling would buy a solid silver teapot, or a prime feather bed, or a mahogany table. One rioter failed to get even a shilling for a splendid mahogany chair, so he smashed it to bits in a fit of temper. Others took their ease on luxurious chairs and sofas while they ate cold legs of mutton and swigged wine from the bottle. So much property had been pillaged that regular convoys of carts and wagons came and went, loaded with spoils. All night long the flames roared, the smoke billowed, the thunder of collapsing roofs and falling walls briefly drowned the drunken cheers and howls and curses, while William III with his cap of liberty stared bleakly down. Mob law ruled Bristol that night.

Few Bristolians (except Colonel Brereton) were in bed. Something like 15,000 or 20,000 spectators were in or around Queen Square. Yet the number of actual rioters – looters and burners – was probably quite small; Samuel Goldney, a surgeon, reckoned there were no more than 100. He went looking for the mayor, and eventually tracked him down at a house in Berkeley Square. The mayor heard his report – it was now 3 a.m. – and wrote a letter to Colonel Brereton, directing him 'to take the most vigorous, effective and decisive measures in your power to quell the existing riot'.

Goldney took this letter to the cavalry stables, where Captain Warrington was technically in command during Brereton's absence. At first Warrington refused to open the letter, then he read it and declined to turn the troops out unless a magistrate came with him. At 4 a.m. one of the aldermen arrived and asked for troops to be sent to Queen Square. Again Warrington dragged his feet: he was willing to act, he said, but the Colonel must give the orders. Together they went to Brereton's lodgings in Unity Street. Two women came to the upper window and denied that Brereton was there, but eventually they got him out of bed. If anything, the commanding officer was more hesitant and rambling than ever. He kept saying that the troops were jaded, the mob was too powerful, and nothing could be done. It took a lot of urging to get him to order his men out, but at last he did it.

The dragoons reached Prince Street as the clock struck five. A warehouse was in flames, with a mob of six or seven hundred around it. The soldiers charged through them and turned into the

Square, where the rioters had just begun to fire the corner house on the south side, belonging to Claxton, a former sheriff. At this point Major Mackworth arrived. He saw the dragoons patrolling the Square in Brereton's usual cautious way, and in effect he took over command of the squadron, calling out: 'Colonel Brereton, we must instantly charge.' Without waiting for an answer, Mackworth shouted, 'Charge, men, and charge home!' It was the beginning of the end of the Bristol Riots.

Mackworth's vigour must have startled Brereton back to life. He charged with great spirit at the head of his men, and they cut the mob to pieces – sabring them down, riding over the bodies, driving them into burning buildings. All the pent-up impatience and resentment of the past 48 hours was suddenly released in a series of thundering, slashing attacks. The squadron charged through the Square, charged back, then re-formed and charged down Prince

The dragoons charge in Queen Square. The beheading
of a rioter has failed to discourage looting of
the houses.

Street, came back to the Square and charged the remnants of the mob again. In the space of a few minutes they killed or wounded about 130 people.

Meanwhile a group of citizens got into Claxton's house, put out the fires and drove out the rioters (who totalled only sixteen, including five women and boys). There were casualties on both sides: a solicitor got two stab-wounds, and Claxton's negro servant threw a rioter clean out of an upstairs window. Mackworth galloped off to Keynsham to recall the 14th Dragoons and, although the rioters made sporadic attacks, Brereton's troops (only 21 of them) held them off until the 14th appeared, together with a dozen men of the Bedminster Yeomanry, who had apparently been sitting out the riots until it was safe to show themselves.

At 7 a.m. Major Beckwith reached Bristol from Gloucester. His unit – also of the 14th Dragoons – was an hour and a half behind him. He found the mayor, several aldermen and the town clerk at the Council House – according to him, all bewildered and stupefied with terror. None of them would come with him, but the mayor gave him written authority to take what action he thought fit. Beckwith went to Queen Square and asked Brereton what on earth had been happening. Brereton offered half a dozen excuses, and went home to change his clothes. Beckwith must have realized that Brereton had lost his grip, because he effectively took over control of the troops.

His own men entered town just as the mob began to reappear. There was an outbreak of plundering at the bishop's palace; again sabres were drawn and blood was spilt. During this diversion, trouble flared up in Queen Square. The 14th Dragoons rode over, formed up in line abreast, charged, and routed the mob, ten or twelve of whom were cut down around the statue of William III. The cavalry swept through into Welsh Back, then split into squads and made separate charges down the Back, along the Grove and into Prince Street. Against pounding hooves and flashing steel the rioters could only run. One gang tried to escape through King Street, only to find it barricaded by constables. The dragoons caught up with the rioters and hacked them to the ground.

Most of the mob escaped into the old city. They were far from beaten and very ready to counterattack. A detachment of the 14th was pelted with stones from the steps of St Nicholas' church until an officer galloped up the steps and cleared the area. The rioters fled through back-alleys and regrouped. The dragoons charged up Clare Street, Corn Street, Wine Street, Peter Street and Castle Street, where they saw a big crowd on Castle Green, all set to march on Queen Square. The cavalry plunged into them, slashing left and right. One soldier reportedly broke two swords and used his scabbard instead. Another is said to have singled out a ringleader – 'a very powerful man' – and beheaded him with a single backhanded cut. The street fighting went on for about two hours, and Mackworth estimated that he saw at least 250 rioters killed or wounded. He may have been right about the number, but they weren't all rioters: several innocent pedestrians got in the troops' way that morning.

It was the end of the serious trouble. There was occasional terrorism on the outskirts, and the cavalry had to pay a visit to St George; but that day the first of a small army reached Bristol. The Tetbury troop of Yeomanry rode in at noon, followed by two troops of North Wilts Yeomanry and two of Somerset Yeomanry from Wells. At 8 p.m. a body of the 11th regiment of foot landed at Shirehampton by steamer from Merthyr. More Yeomanry came in from Frome and Wincanton. The Government instructed part of the 52nd regiment to proceed with all speed from Portsmouth; at the same time a brigade of artillery was rushed from Woolwich. Orders also went out to send troops from Dublin, Waterford, Cork, Pembroke and Plymouth. Frigates were moved to the Bristol Channel. Now that it was all over – and now that 4,000 special constables were on duty – the authorities were taking no chances.

The entire disaster had lasted less than three days. It took a lot longer to clear up the mess. The ruins in Queen Square were searched for bodies; astonishingly, one man was dug out of the vaults, alive, but with an arm burnt off above the elbow. (He is said to have walked away.) The search for looted property went on for many days, at first in Marsh Street (the Irish quarter), then in Lewins Mead, Host Street, St James's, the Pithay, the Dings, Baptist Mills, Bedminster and Kingswood. Many houses were found to be crammed with stolen goods. Forty wagonloads were brought in; the stuff overflowed the quadrangle of the Exchange and had to be stacked in the parish churches. It was dug up in back yards, hauled out of wells, pulled out of pigsties, salvaged from the Float and the Avon. An Irishman was caught wearing three shirts, three jackets and three pairs of trousers. An apparently expectant mother turned out to have two silk waistcoats and a pair of blankets stuffed up her front. A man called Ives took a massive silver salver, the property of the Corporation, and cut it into 169 bits; but the silversmith to whom he offered a piece was suspicious, and Ives

Somebody had to pay. Four rioters are hanged at the New Gaol (whose gates still stand today). It was an unpopular site for executions - too near the river for a lot of spectators to get a good view.

got fourteen years' transportation. (The silversmith put the salver together again, and fourteen years later Ives called at the Council House and asked to see it.)

There were more arrests: 127 in all. Just to prove that they had learnt nothing and forgotten nothing, the Corporation proposed that the rioters should be tried before Sir Charles Wetherell. Fortunately the Government knew better. On 2nd January 1832 a Special Commission opened in the Guildhall before the Lord Chief Justice (Sir Nicholas Conyngham Tyndal), two judges and the Duke of Beaufort, who was lord high steward of Bristol. The trials lasted twelve days. Charges against twenty-five prisoners were dropped. Eighty-one of the remaining 102 were found guilty. Forty-three got various terms of imprisonment with hard labour; six got seven years' transportation; one – Ives – got fourteen years, twenty-six got 'technical' death sentences but in fact were transported for life. The remaining five – Christopher Davis, William Clarke, Thomas Gregory, Joseph Kayes and Richard Vines – were condemned to death. Vines was obviously a mental defective; his sentence was commuted to transportation for life. The other four men were hanged above the scorched entrance of the New Gaol, at midday, on Friday, 27th January 1832, in the presence of a very large crowd.

One of the condemned men, Christopher Davis, was a particularly sad case. He was a normally respectable, lower-middle-class citizen who had a weak head: a few drinks sent him haywire. Although he himself did nothing violent, he cheered the rioters too loud and long for his own good. Men who were more destructive, but less conspicuous, escaped; Davis suffered for their crimes as well as his own. Another prisoner who never stood a chance was Clarke. His counsel, Mr Palmer, tried to persuade the court to acquit him of felony because 'if he had been proved guilty of any crime, it was of high treason'. Palmer lost his point, and his client lost his life.

After the trials came the courts-martial. Captain Warrington was found guilty on charges which arose out of his refusal to obey the mayor's written orders in the early hours of Monday morning. He was cashiered, but gently – they allowed him to sell his commission, which had a market value of upwards of £3,225.

But Warrington's fate had already been overshadowed by Brereton's. Eleven charges were made against Brereton, and the weight of evidence was crushing. General Dalbiac, the prosecuting officer, began by describing the degree of blame as 'altogether unprecedented and unheard of in the case of a British officer'. The witnesses came and went; the court carefully reconstructed all that Brereton had done, or not done; and steadily the full, horrifying measure of his failure became clear. Brereton had done as much damage as any hundred rioters.

On the fourth day of the court-martial the evidence was especially damning. The court heard how Brereton had sent the 14th Dragoons to Keynsham (*'Lieutenant-Colonel Brereton came to me a second time, and said, "For God's sake, Captain Gage, will you get out of town?"'*); how he had fraternized with the mob (*'I saw Lieutenant-Colonel Brereton . . . take off his hat and huzza to the mob …'*); above all, how Cornet Kelson's troop had gone to the New Gaol when it was attacked, and had come straight back (*'He asked me what I had done at the gaol; I said I had done what he told me – nothing.'*).

Brereton returned home late that night: about eleven o'clock. He always kissed his daughters – one was three, the other six – before he went to bed. Brereton was a widower, and the girls slept in the housekeeper's bedroom, so she waited up until he had visited the children. That night Brereton sat up until three in the morning, and he never did kiss his daughters goodnight. Instead, he went to his room, lay on his bed, and shot himself through the heart.

CHAPTER SIX

CRUSTED PORT

Claud Cockburn once thought of writing a book on the English, to be called *How About Wednesday Week?*, that being the English idea of urgency. Any history of the port of Bristol since 1700 should be called *How About The Year After Next?* It's the story of generation upon generation of long-winded, short-sighted men who talked too much, did too little, and left that little so late that the rest of the shipping world nearly gave Bristol up as a bad job.

By 1755 Bristol had been the second biggest port in the country for so long that its citizens seemed to think the world owed them a living. At first glance the port still looked healthily full of ships – but only during high tide; when the tide went out it looked dangerously full of ships. Bristol still had no wet dock – only a series of quays and wharves – so at low water there was nowhere for the ships to go but down on to the steeply cambered mud-banks. It did them no good: 'complaints have frequently arisen that ships of burthen, by lying aground ... when the tide is out ... have had their timbers so strained that it was found necessary to send them to dock to repair the damages', reported a committee of the Corporation.

And that wasn't all. The port itself was too small; shipping was often dangerously crowded. When the tide was out there was always a risk that fire might spread from ship to ship; even when the tide was in, ships trying to leave port sometimes had trouble squeezing out. The committee's message was clear: Bristol's port was inadequate. The Corporation did nothing.

That was in 1755. Forty-six years *earlier*, Liverpool had begun work on a 'floating dock'; by now it had two of them – ample, permanently wet berthing where ships could load or unload at any stage of the tide; and Liverpool's docks weren't placed at the top of a twisting, eight-mile river. In those days, every ship that went to Bristol had to be towed up the Avon by teams of rowing boats, and later towed down again. The harbour itself was no Shangri-La: most sewage and rubbish ended up there, and the water was rich with 'blood, garbage, stinking meat, dogs, cats, etc.' There had to be a better way of doing things, and Bristol should have learned from Liverpool before the competition grew hot. Bristol didn't.

In August 1757 the Corporation set up another committee to look at the docks. This one never reported back, but maybe somebody had heard of Liverpool, because in February 1758 the Town Clerk advertised for engineers to design a wet dock. Nothing came of this, probably because the Corporation changed its mind and decided it wasn't going to have a wet dock after all. That being the case, it quickly defused a private plan put forward by a group of merchants who wanted to build one, by coming up with an alternative idea.

The Corporation had already leased to the Merchant Venturers' Society the right to collect dues for using the quays and wharves. Now the Corporation did a deal: if the Society would enlarge the quays and wharves at its own expense, this lease would be re-negotiated. Six years later (nobody was in any great hurry) a new, 99-year lease was signed by which the Merchant Venturers paid the Corporation £10 a year rental. Extending the quays cost the Society no more than £10,000, which they probably got back within five or six years; certainly their income from dues had passed the £2,000-a-year mark by 1787. The Merchant Venturers did very well out of that deal. So, of course, did some of the Corporation; they were Merchant Venturers too.

Meanwhile, all the old problems remained. In fact they increased, because the size of merchant ships was steadily increasing. The strain which they placed on the port – and the strain which the mud banks placed on *them* – was very obvious. All the same, nothing else was done in that century. For the next 35 years Bristol dozed, while Liverpool boomed.

Occasionally there was a flicker of interest, but the enthusiasts wasted their energy on criticism of each other's ideas. In 1767 a local engineer called Champion planned a floating dock and estimated the cost at £30,000. His opponents hired Mylne, a rival engineer. Mylne disliked the plan and said it would cost £60,000. That killed Champion's chances and discouraged further discussion for 20 years.

In 1787 the Merchant Venturers' Society was shown a new scheme for a floating dock, price £25,000, prepared by a Mr Nickalls. This produced more argument than agreement, so the Society called in another engineer, Jessop, who told them that Nickalls' scheme would cost £30,000, and drew up his own design. Before long a third engineer, Smeaton, got into the act. Smeaton dismissed both Nickalls' and Jessop's proposals and tabled a £74,500 plan of his own. The Venturers – no doubt dazzled by three lots of science – passed the whole lot over to the Corporation and strongly recommended that something be done, and the Corporation appointed a committee to consider the situation.

Appointing a committee is all too often the kiss of death, or at least the kiss of paralysis. Nothing happened for the next four years.

Then, in December 1791, the committee reported to the Corporation that it endorsed the Merchant Venturers' scheme (which one, isn't revealed) and in a burst of energy the Corporation ordered its committee to contact the Society and take the whole thing a stage further. Less than two years later the committee was back. Its recommendation: that the Corporation should promote an Act of Parliament for improving the port of Bristol. At last there was a prospect of action.

Nothing happened.

Eight years later – in July 1801 – the Merchant Venturers enquired what, if anything, had been done. This seems to have jolted the Corporation awake. Jessop set to work on new plans, and in May 1802 the Society and Corporation jointly published them. A year later Parliament passed an Act which authorized the work and approved the setting up of a Bristol Dock Company to do it. On 1st May 1804, at the unceremonial hour of 5 a.m., the first sod was turned for the digging of the New Cut – 95 years after Liverpool began work on *its* docks.

One consolation was the scale of the work, which was impressive. Two miles of the old bed of the Avon and Frome were to be converted into a Floating Harbour (soon shortened to 'Float') with lock gates at Cumberland Basin, two new bridges, and the

New Cut – a man-made channel two miles long, through which the Avon would be diverted from Totterdown to Hotwells. At the top end a feeder canal would be dug to top up the Float and link it with the Avon and Kennet Canal. There would also be a new sewer to cope with 'the greatest part of the Sewage at present discharged into the Avon above Bristol-bridge, from whence the Brewers and Distillers are mostly supplied', which makes you stop and think a bit.

The whole project carried a price tag of £300,000. Luckily the Napoleonic wars provided cheap labour in the form of French prisoners-of-war (Stapleton prison held 5,500 of them), but the New Cut alone was a hefty task: the excavation had to bite deep into the rock. The Dock Company ran out of money. Parliament passed a second Act. Still the Company over-spent. A third Bill was thrown out in 1807, re-written and passed in 1808. The Company ran into expensive trouble; in February 1809 its new Bath Bridge collapsed, and killed two workmen. Parliament had to rescue the operation with a fourth Act. When the Floating Harbour was finished it had cost £580,000.

The directors celebrated with a massive blowout for the labourers. One thousand men sat down to an open-air dinner in the fields between the Cut and the Float. Watched by 'a vast concourse of spectators' they put away (amongst other things) two oxen roasted whole, six hundredweight of plum pudding and a thousand gallons of stingo. All went well until the Irish contingent intercepted a cart loaded with fresh ale and 'unceremoniously disburthened the vehicle of its contents'. Their English colleagues questioned their right to do this. A hundred Irishmen departed for their lodgings in Marsh Street, collected shillelaghs, met the English in Prince Street, and enjoyed a colossal dust-up until the police came and cut it short.

It was an appropriate start for the Float. The next 40 years were to see plenty of strife in and around Bristol Dock Company.

One big problem was there from the start. The new dock worked beautifully, but it had cost too much. The directors had raised the money by promising fat dividends – 8 per cent was the figure usually mentioned – and now they couldn't pay. During their first fifteen years in business they paid no dividend at all; in 1823 they paid 1 per cent; for the next 20 years it averaged under 2¼ per cent. This was all very awkward. The Company could think of only one way to make more money, and that was to put up their charges. Unhappily, they put them up so much that they frightened a lot of ships away.

Creating the Float should have done the port of Bristol a power of good. In fact, all that happened was that Bristol's trade stopped going backwards in comparison with the other ports, and stayed more or less stationary for the next 20 or 30 years. The fault lay in particular with the Dock Company, which was incompetent; with the Corporation, which was stiffnecked and greedy; and with the Merchant Venturers, who had gone to sleep. In general the fault lay with the system of local government, which was medieval: the men in power represented nobody but themselves.

By 1823 things were so bad that local merchants and manufacturers got together and founded the Chamber of Commerce, with one aim: reform of the port. Matthew Gooch, editor of *Felix Farley's Bristol Journal,* spelled out a few home truths:

'Take for instance the export of woollen goods from this city, seated in the very heart of the clothing manufactures of Gloucestershire and Somersetshire. What is the amount of woollen goods that have been exported for the last year? To compare the same with Liverpool, Hull, Whitehaven, even with any little fishing town … is indeed a mortifying subject. When Liverpool is yearly exporting her tens of thousands of yards of woollen goods, we are exporting our hundreds: and all due to our town dues and mayor's dues and heavy local taxation. And what, think you, is the amount of teas exported in the last twelve months from the port of Bristol? Liverpool is exporting to Ireland at least 5,000 chests and half-chests; Bristol, within 40 hours sail of the capital of the sister kingdom, has exported during the year 124 lbs weight.'

He had much the same to say of Bristol's timber trade, which had moved to Gloucester and Chepstow, and the iron trade, with which 'the little town of Newport is fast rising upon our ruins'.

Gooch was right: Bristol's taxes were killing local commerce and industry. The Chamber of Commerce added up the port dues payable on 44 different articles of merchandise, and found that the figure was more than twice what it was in London, Liverpool or Hull. Some charges were so enormous that it was virtually impossible for any Bristol firm to deal in those goods. For instance, on indigo (widely used by west-country textile factories) the port of Bristol's charge was *seventeen times* as much as London's.

The Chamber of Commerce presented its findings to the Corporation. The evidence was, you would think, overwhelming. For example, the seven most heavily taxed items were almonds, bees-wax, cochineal, ivory, indigo, linen and silk. Calculating the total port charges on the city's average annual import of these seven items, compared with what the charges would be in other ports, produced these startling figures:

	£	s	d
London	42	4	2
Hull	30	14	2
Gloucester	22	2	11
Bristol	614	8	9

The Corporation declined to be startled. They passed a resolution reproaching the Chamber of Commerce for its hasty and unkind opinions. The Chamber was in no mood to back down, and it made remarks about how the municipal charters 'hath through mismanagement been perverted to her (Bristol's) degredation'. The Corporation then played its own smooth version of the three-card trick. It announced that, if everybody agreed that town dues and port charges were seriously harming trade, the Corporation would 'most readily' promote legal measures 'to modify and reduce such town dues and port charges so that they shall in no case amount to more on any specific article than the sum now collected'. Somebody remarked that it reminded him of the time when the Kingswood miners stormed into town demanding that bread should be cheaper. 'If,' said the mayor, 'you'll go home peaceably, you shall have a 12-

penny loaf for a shilling.' On that occasion it worked (or so they say); however the Chamber of Commerce knew how many pence made twelve, and they pressed the Corporation to cut its charges, in particular the town dues and mayor's dues, which they blamed for 'the languor and comparative decline of Bristol trade'.

The Corporation fought stubbornly. These dues, they insisted, belonged to them as of right; they owned them, like property. They even tried to get Parliament to pass a Bill confirming this. The Chamber of Commerce attacked the Council on the grounds that it was self-elected (and therefore irresponsible); it didn't spend the dues it collected on anything of benefit to Bristol (such as improving the streets); it never published accounts; and in general it behaved as if these public funds were none of the public's business. The Corporation's answer boiled down to this: 'Quite right – it is none of your business.' But the rumpus was so loud that a Government Commission came down to investigate, and eventually the Corporation had to give way. Town dues and mayor's dues were cut by two-fifths. It was better than nothing, but it wasn't nearly enough.

Nor was the energy of the Dock Company directors enough. The summer of 1825 turned out to be very hot, and the Float stank like it had never stunk before. Nearly six miles of sewers drained into it. Most of the muck didn't drain out, and the hot weather brought it bubbling to the surface, 'a stagnant mass of putridity', as one newspaper called it. The stench made strong men shudder and weak men reel, but as usual the Dock Company ignored all complaints.

For once the suffering citizens organized themselves. The Act of Parliament which authorized the Float had made the Dock Company responsible for getting rid of sewage, and a writ was taken out to compel the directors to do this. First they denied all responsibility, then they dragged their feet, finally and grudgingly they built a culvert to divert the Frome (which was virtually a sewer) into the New Cut, where the stench persisted in living memory, as any resident of Coronation Road would confirm on a warm day.

It all went to show just how little sympathy Bristolians could expect from the directors or, for that matter, from the Corporation. Port charges were still cripplingly high – so high, in fact, that in 1828 one local businessman challenged the Corporation to prove its right to claim them. He lost his case and the Corporation kept its money, but anybody with eyes in his head could see that the port was losing business at a rate of knots.

Bristol's exports in 1822 were worth £315,000. By 1833 they had fallen to £205,000, and the Float was beginning to look empty. Warehouse space was going begging. Bristol was in a slump, and the Chamber of Commerce hammered away at the cause. In July 1834 the Dock Company did in fact reduce a few of its charges, but only on relatively trivial items: their rates on major goods were still far heavier than Liverpool's – sugar 50 per cent more, tobacco 70 per cent more, wine 157 per cent more, foreign spirits 200 per cent more, and wool a suicidal 1,100 per cent more. The Chamber of Commerce made a survey of the port dues charged for 23 major items, ranging from cheese and cotton to wine and ivory. Here they are, converted to modern currency. For every £1 collected by Bristol, Liverpool collected only 57p, London 52p, Hull 36p, and Gloucester 31p. Bristol charged 50p a bale on silk; Gloucester charged 3p. The wonder was that any skipper in his right mind used the port of Bristol at all.

But by this time the House of Commons, which had just reformed itself, was keen to reform the country's municipal corporations too. In 1833 a royal commission went out to take a long close look at them. Bristol Corporation was annoyed and offended. The local Establishment was indignant that this 'Radical Inquisition' should have the nerve to poke its nose into the purely private matter of local government – or, as it turned out, local misgovernment. The Merchant Venturers (probably the stuffiest and most self-satisfied men in Bristol) and the Dock Company refused to have anything to do with the enquiry. The Corporation had enough sense not to resist it, and in their report the commissioners quietly and methodically tore the Corporation to pieces.

Mismanagement and extravagance were the main charges. 'With

a sinking and overburdened trade,' the report said acidly, 'its large revenues have been unprofitably expended in the maintenance of an overgrown establishment, and in the display of state magnificence ...'. There was no lack of evidence of this. The mayor's salary had just been dropped from £2,000 to £1,604 with a recommendation to cut down on banquets because the city was so deep in debt. (At one point the mayor's salary had reached £2,500, and that of the sheriffs £1,260 a year.) The Corporation had spent £925 on a civic reception for the Duke of Wellington, £1,225 on a four-hour visit by the Prince of Wales, and £1,396 on giving Lord Grenville the freedom of the city. (To get the modern value of these sums, multiply by 75.) A quarter or more of all the civic income went on eating, drinking and display.

All this pomp and stuffing was well and good when it came out of the overflow of prosperity; but – as the commissioners stressed – the Corporation had done a rotten job of looking after the economy of Bristol. 'Far below her former station as the second port of the empire,' they sniffed, 'she now has to sustain a mortifying competition with second-rate ports in her own Channel.' They slammed the Corporation for making a gift of the wharfage dues to the Merchant Venturers and for stacking so many charges on trade that they had broken its back. They concluded that there was 'something essentially bad' in the way Bristol was governed.

It meant the end of the old Corporation. One of the last acts of the Council was to abolish town dues on exports. (Too late: exports had shrunk almost to nothing; they raised only £466 in 1834.) The reformed Corporation elected in 1836 was a far more intelligent and responsible body, but the dead hands of the Dock Company and the Merchant Venturers' Society still lay on the port. The royal commissioners had made it clear that the port of Bristol was far too expensive, and that as long as Bristol charged 44s. 9d. to handle a ton of coal while London charged 15s. 1d., the city would get no more than the miserable business it deserved. The Dock Company still refused to see the logic of this. Dividends, it said, came first.

In any case, a much bigger problem than port dues was rapidly coming over the horizon. *The port was in the wrong place.*

In a sense, it had always been in the wrong place. To be towed eight miles up a twisting, tidal river and through a narrow, rocky gorge is not the ideal finish to any captain's voyage. When the Romans wanted a ferry terminal for South Wales they picked a spot much closer to the mouth of the Avon: Sea Mills harbour. (In 1712 there was a short-lived attempt to build a dock there again.) The eight-mile trip up or down the river was not only tedious and costly, it was dangerous. Down through the centuries, wrecks and groundings have been commonplace. In March 1579 the *Lion,* a large merchant vessel, struck some rocks in the Avon and sank, fully laden. She couldn't be refloated, and in the end they had to tear her to bits. The tideway was blocked for over a year.

That was in Elizabeth's reign. By Victoria's time the Avon was a far bigger problem, because ships themselves were three or four times bigger. By the 1820s steamers were operating, although Bristol gave them little encouragement. Despite the fact that passenger sailing ships often took six weeks to get from Bristol to Cork, it wasn't until 1822 that the first steamboat service began on this route; and by then steamers from Holyhead and Liverpool had won a near-monopoly of the Irish run. Bristol's suspicion of steam tugs was even worse. If ever a river cried out for steam towing it was the Avon. Bristol persisted in using men in row-boats or horses on the bank, at a cost of £9 per tow for a 100-ton vessel. The Clyde had steam tugs in 1803, and the Tyne, Mersey and Thames followed shortly after; it was 1836 before Bristol saw her first steam tug, the *Fury.* Her arrival caused riots in Pill, where the towing crews lived. One night, when she was off Portishead, 30 of them boarded her at gunpoint, forced the captain and crew into a small boat, tried to scuttle the *Fury,* and finally set her adrift.

One organization did recognize the advantages of steam: the Chamber of Commerce. Its members realized that steamers offered regular, reliable sailings, and in 1828 they urged the Government to establish Bristol as a mail-packet station for Ireland. The Government made the obvious reply: Bristol was in no position to offer daily sailings at fixed times.

That was the problem in a nutshell. The location of the docks made them always difficult, and sometimes impossible, to approach or leave; and the situation could only get worse. The obvious solution was to put them somewhere else. A letter to the *Bristol Journal* of 1st February 1823 points out that even at Pill there isn't always enough water, and suggests that a landing-place should be built nearer the river's mouth, where 'I have no doubt but Steam Packets of moderate burthen could arrive and depart at all states of the tide'. He adds that the Corporation owned the land, and although the Shirehampton-Bristol road was hilly, a road could easily be made to follow the river to Hotwells.

Whoever that writer was, he had his head screwed on: he anticipated Avonmouth docks by 50 years, and the Portway by 100. The pity is that so few other people had his vision. Most Bristolians were incapable of looking beyond their own city centre. It was as if they had taken so long to get their Floating Harbour that they couldn't believe it was already obsolescent. So Bristol sat waiting for the world to sail eight miles up the Avon, as it always had done. It took the city far too long to admit that times had changed, and that it was up to Bristol to adapt to the world, not *vice versa;* and by then most of the business had gone elsewhere, for good.

After the Government's rebuff, the Chamber of Commerce invited the Merchant Venturers to join them and erect a pier at Avonmouth. For some reason the Society was feeling huffy towards the Chamber, and all it said was that it had already suggested building a pier near the Lamplighter's Hotel at Shirehampton: a reply worthy of a child of six. The Chamber kept pushing its idea, and after a while the Society leaned down from its high horse long enough to say that in its opinion an Avonmouth pier would be *(a)* costly and *(b)* not profitable; but if the Corporation and the Dock Company joined in, the Society might consider the scheme. Then the riots and reforms of the early 1830s came along and put a stop to all such plans. When Brunel suggested a pier at Portishead to service the Irish mailboats, nobody could agree on anything, and he abandoned it.

Meanwhile, the railways were coming. A rail link with London had tremendous implications for Bristol; it was yet another reason for creating a new port where ships of all sizes could dock at any stage of the tide. Brunel saw the exciting potential of Bristol as a transatlantic terminus – the perfect link between trains to and from London and ships to and from America. In 1836 the Great Western Steamship Company was founded and Brunel began work on the first-ever purpose-built Atlantic steamer, the *Great Western*.

She was launched in Bristol in 1837: at 1,370 tons the biggest boat the Avon had ever seen. Next year she sailed from Bristol to New York in 14 days 16 hours and back again in 12 days 14 hours; what mattered as much as her speed was her economy in fuel. The *Great Western* was a maritime triumph and a business success; she was just what Bristol needed to restore glamour and trade to the port. Yet, looking back, it almost seems as if the city was trying to drive the *Great Western* away.

Obviously the harbour was too small for her to use regularly, so she had to anchor off Avonmouth and transfer passengers and cargo by small boats. For this the Dock Company charged £106 a time, plus as much again for cargo dues; their attitude was that they didn't see why they should be deprived of their profits just because the ship owners had built a vessel too large to get into their dock.

Even so, if Brunel's plan to make a long pier at Portishead had come off, the *Great Western* might have gone on using Bristol. When the Dock Company refused to lower its dues, a joint committee representing the Corporation, the Merchant Venturers and the Steamship Company met to try and work out a solution. They called in Brunel to advise them. He recommended widening the entrance to the Float, building a new dock no higher than Sea Mills, and creating a pier at Portishead. The Dock Company refused to consider any of it. In February 1842 the Steamship Company decided that the *Great Western* should sail alternately from Bristol and Liverpool (they saved £200 a voyage by using Liverpool); not long afterwards, she stopped coming to Bristol altogether.

The farcical aspect of all this was the Dock Company's dimwitted devotion to dividends. Year after year they drove away trade by charging too much and spending too little, all in the cause of paying their shareholders; and year after year the shareholders got back peanuts. From 1823 to 1844 the Company paid an annual dividend which averaged less than 2¼ per cent. In 1845 and 1846 it paid no dividend at all. The Corporation had offered to take over the Company and pay regular interest at 2¼ per cent on all shares, but the directors wanted more. In 1845 the Corporation offered 2½ per cent. The directors demanded 3 per cent. The Corporation suggested going to arbitration. The directors weren't interested. The Corporation gave up.

This was sheer bloody-mindedness on the part of the Dock Company. The port was in trouble, and they knew it. Bristol's export trade had taken a disastrous dive – from £340,000 in 1839 to £150,000 in 1846 – partly because the port was too expensive, and partly because of the disaster of the *Great Britain*.

The S.S. Great Britain was magnificent - and far too big to use the port of Bristol. Here she is in full sail; evidently Brunel's steam engines needed some help.

Today most people think of Brunel's masterpiece as a sort of Bristolian triumph. The *Great Britain* was a triumph of design and construction, and most of the credit for that goes to Brunel; but from the moment she was launched she became a floating advertisement for Liverpool.

She was *three times* the size of the *Great Western*. If the smaller ship couldn't use the city docks, where did Bristol expect this monster to go? The Steamship Company has been criticized for giving Brunel his head and spending too much time and money on a huge and revolutionary new steamer, when it could have built a whole fleet of *Great Westerns* and taken a grip on the transatlantic trade. As it was – so the argument goes – Sam Cunard saw his chance and had four *Great Western*-type Cunarders in service from Liverpool by the time the *Great Britain* was ready to sail. This criticism misses the point by a mile. Even if the Steamship Company had built a dozen duplicates of the *Great Western*, Bristol still hadn't so much as a pier where they could tie up, let alone a dock where they could be serviced. The port of Bristol had been built at a time when ocean-going ships averaged maybe 400 tons, and 800 tons was big. The *Great Western* was 1,340 tons, the *Great Britain*, 3,270 tons. Bristol financed them, built them, launched them, cheered them, and then watched them sail away to Liverpool. It was the only place they could go.

Then bad luck completed the damage which bad judgement had begun. In September 1846, on her second transatlantic voyage, the *Great Britain* went aground in Dundrum Bay, Co. Down. She lay stranded for eleven months before her owners refloated her, badly damaged. They had to sell her for £18,000, a loss of £107,896. The works where she was built had to go, too: the firm lost another £47,277 on that. The disaster struck the company a fatal blow; most shares were a complete write-off. Confidence in Bristol was badly shaken.

Failure, of course, was the Dock Company's middle name by now. In 1846 the businessmen of Bristol launched a massive and well-organized campaign against the Company, through a new body: the Free Port Association. Their case was simple: while other ports went forward, Bristol stood still. Why? Because a vessel entering the port of Bristol was charged 2s. 7d. a ton compared with 9½ d. a ton at London, 3½ d. at Southampton, 3d. at Cardiff and nothing at all at Gloucester; because Bristol's import charges were roughly twice as much as Liverpool's, three times as much as Gloucester's, seven times as much as Cardiff's. The Free Port Association wanted to liberate Bristol from 'the obnoxious dues and charges that have so long oppressed us' so that 'the energies and exertions of our rising citizens will be no longer crippled as they have been for the last thirty years'.

The Association held meetings all over the city, hammering home the message of the damage done by the Dock Company's immovable, unthinking selfishness: damage to the sugar trade, loss of timber imports, many businesses at a standstill, a total of 536 tenements standing vacant, rents worth £10,000 a year lost, and so on. Further evidence stood next to the docks: 'Good manufacturing waterside premises, costing £22,000 and mortgaged in 1832 for £5,000, had been sold in 1846 for £3,100.'

After two years of constant pressure, the Association won. The directors agreed terms, and on 23rd August 1848 the Corporation formally took over the docks. The deal was financed by a fourpenny rate, despite furious opposition from the property-owners of Clifton, who didn't see why they should have anything to do with Bristol, its grubby trade or its squalid docks.

The new Docks Committee took an axe to the port charges. They removed all dues on 530 types of merchandise, trimmed the rest by an average 20 per cent and cut the charge on ships by half. At once the port began to recover. Trade picked up so well that, three years later, the Docks Committee reported a surplus of £3,800, and cut its charges even more. In the ten years after the takeover, Bristol's import trade climbed by 62 per cent. The reduced dock dues brought in 50 per cent *more* revenue than before – enough to pay a nice dividend, if dividends had been paid. One wonders what the ex-directors thought as they looked at themselves in their shaving-mirrors each morning. Nothing, perhaps: thinking had never been their strong suit.

At long last the port of Bristol was being managed intelligently and profitably, and it was attracting its share of those ships which could get into the Float. But the physical obstacles remained, and got worse as the years went by. The Float was still too far inland, it was still too small for many ships, and ships were still getting bigger and bigger. (By 1855 Brunel was designing the *Great Eastern*, 22,000 tons.) And on 10th November 1851 an accident happened which should have jolted every Bristol trader into seeing the absolute necessity for another dock at Avonmouth.

The *Demerara* was a brand new paddle steamer of about 3,000 tons, the biggest ship ever launched in Bristol except for the *Great Britain*. She left Cumberland Basin in tow of a Glasgow tug, which was to take her to the Clyde for engine-fitting. They were late, and the tide had begun to ebb; the tug set off at 7 or 8 miles an hour – dangerously fast in those narrow waters. The *Demerara's* bow smashed into the rocky bank below the Sea Walls, the tide swung her broadside across the stream, and the stern slammed against the opposite bank. As the tideway emptied, the ship settled, and twisted. For a few scarifying hours it looked as if the wreck was a total loss and the port was sealed off, but desperate efforts got her afloat and she was hauled away. Nevertheless, the warning was clear – to the owners of big ships, if not to Bristol itself: a port eight miles up a narrow river was a liability. Bristol had spent the first half of the century repeating, three times a day before breakfast, that what was good enough for Canynge and Cabot was still good enough for the likes of Brunel and Cunard. How much longer would the city take to learn the truth?

Another twenty-six years.

Those years are a dreary serial of discarded plans, endless committees, caution, timidity, rivalry, jealousy, accidents, delays and – almost incredibly – eventual success.

In 1852, after the wreck of the *Demerara*, a group of citizens commissioned a design for an ocean steam dock at Avonmouth (which was then just barren land). The estimated cost – a million and a half - killed that scheme. In 1853 two plans were put

*The S.S. Demerara aground in the Avon Gorge, blocking the river
and sealing off the port - which was in the wrong place.*

forward: one for a gigantic double dock at Pill, the other for a
Portishead dock; both sank without trace. In 1857 the Great
Eastern Steamship Company supported a scheme for docks at the
river's mouth; that one went into a joint committee and was never
seen again. In 1858 an elaborate plan for 'dockizing' the whole
river appeared and disappeared, along with various other projects
for piers and landing-stages.

In 1860 they were still talking, and some of what they said
explains why they weren't doing anything. Although Avonmouth
didn't yet exist, Bristol was already afraid of it. Sir John Hawkshaw
reported to the Council that docks for ocean steamers could be
made down there but he was agin it: 'docks at the river's mouth
would encourage the growth of population in the immediate
neighbourhood, and would lead in the first place to a divided trade
and ultimately to a competitive trade'. It never occurred to Sir John
that if Avonmouth didn't get the trade, Bristol certainly wouldn't,

nor that Avonmouth's trade might be made to benefit the city. His eyesight reached to the city boundaries and no further.

Next year – 1861 – the Council voted against raising money through the rates for financing ocean-steamers at Avonmouth. Yet when a private company – the Port Railway & Pier Co. – asked Parliament for powers to build a pier at Avonmouth linked by a railway line to Hotwells, the Corporation opposed them and the Bill was defeated. In 1862 the company had better luck, and two years later the pier and railway were opened.

By this time a rival company – the Bristol & Portishead Pier & Railway Co. – had been formed. *Their* railway and pier were in action by 1868, and the rivalry grew into a three-way fight between those who wanted a dock at Avonmouth, those who wanted one at Portishead, and those who detested the thought of having any port outside Bristol. Building either of the new docks was bound to cost a packet, so this fierce competition for investors' money only made life more difficult for both of them. After all those years without a big, modern dock, the prospect of having two of the beasts provoked endless argument and strife. The whole thing, said the *Bristol Times,* was 'like a sort of nightmare on the society of the city'. The paper described the struggle as 'of a character to break up old acquaintances, to chill conviviality, to make men look pale and spiteful at one another when it was introduced at table ...'

To add ammunition to the fight, there was yet another disaster on the Avon. In November 1866 the Cardiff tug *Black Eagle* had a ship under tow near St Vincent's Rocks when the tug's boiler burst. The captain was blown on to the bank, and people saw chunks of the boiler hurled higher than the deck of the Suspension Bridge; later, a 4-cwt piece was found in a garden nearly 300 feet above where the tug had been.

The wreck of the *Black Eagle* could be described as an Act of God; the wreck of the *Kron Prinz* was like the *Demerara* all over again, only worse.

The *Kron Prinz* had a cargo of 7,000 quarters of barley from the Danube. She came up the Avon at high water on 1st April

1874, failed to get round the Horseshoe Bend and ploughed into the bank a few hundred yards below Sea Mills station. For three weeks they heaved and strained at her, but she just lay on her side and spilled barley by the ton up and down the banks. Eventually the combined efforts of men, tugs and tide pulled her off. The loss came to £34,000. (Just to rub it in, a steamer called the *Gypsy* ran aground near Blackrock Quarry four years later; she was a total wreck.)

The publicity was bad for business, and it was just as well that the other docks were nearly ready. They too had had their share of accidents. Avonmouth dock was begun in 1868 but the company ran out of money and had to stop work, much to the delight of its Portishead rivals, who were a couple of years behind. In 1873 the Avonmouth company got going again. In 1874 a high tide collapsed the dyke at Portishead which held back the Severn; water flooded the dock workings and the Portishead company lost eighteen months. Avonmouth won back its lead: the dock was opened in 1877. Portishead aimed at an 1878 opening, but a great length of dock wall collapsed, and the repairs weren't finished until 1879.

Once the docks began operating, of course, the port of Bristol felt the draught. Many ships abandoned the tortuous trip up the Avon and went straight into Avonmouth or Portishead instead. Inevitably there was a fair amount of teeth-gnashing over this competition – somebody described Portishead as 'a daughter seeking to cut the throat of her mother' – but after only five years of wrangling and name-calling, the city did the obvious thing and bought both Avonmouth and Portishead docks.

The date was 1st September 1884. The port of Bristol had finally dragged itself, twitching and spluttering, into the nineteenth century – with just fifteen years and four months to spare.